A
Maryknoll
Book of
Prayer

A
Maryknoll
Book of
Prayer

Michael Leach and Susan Perry, editors

ORBIS BOOKS

Maryknoll, New York 10545

Second printing, March 2003

Founded in 1970, Orbis Books endeavors to publish works that enlighten the mind, nourish the spirit, and challenge the conscience. The publishing arm of the Maryknoll Fathers & Brothers, Orbis seeks to explore the global dimensions of the Christian faith and mission, to invite dialogue with diverse cultures and religious traditions, and to serve the cause of reconciliation and peace. The books published reflect the views of their authors and do not represent the official position of the Maryknoll Society. To learn more about Maryknoll and Orbis Books, please visit our website at www.maryknoll.org.

Manufactured in the United States of America.
Manuscript editing and typesetting by Joan Weber Laflamme.

Library of Congress Cataloging-in-Publication Data

A Maryknoll book of prayer / Michael Leach and Susan Perry, editors.
  p. cm.
Includes index.
 ISBN 1-57075-447-0 (paper)
 1. Prayers. I. Leach, Michael, 1940- II. Perry, Susan.
 BV210.3 .M37 2003
 242'.802—dc21

2002011007

Psalm 86:6–12

Give ear, O LORD, to my prayer;
   listen to the sound of my supplication.
In the day of my trouble I call on you,
   for you will answer me.

There is none like you among the gods, O LORD,
   nor are there any works like yours.
All the nations you have made shall come
   and bow down before you, O LORD,
   and shall glorify your name.
For you are great and do wondrous things;
   you alone are God.
Teach me your way, O LORD,
   that I may walk in your truth;
   give me an undivided heart to revere your name.
I give thanks to you, O LORD my God, with my whole
      heart,
   and I will glorify your name forever.

In Gratitude

To Barbara Hussey Riggins
whose love and enthusiasm
made this book possible

and,
in appreciation
of all the supporters of Maryknoll
whose generosity she represents
and who make Maryknoll possible

Contents

Introduction

When I was crossing into Gaza, I was asked at the checkpoint whether I was carrying any weapons. I replied: "Oh yes, my prayer books."

MOTHER TERESA

When we asked the members of the Maryknoll family to send us their favorite prayers, little did we know that our office would look like the courtroom in one of the final scenes of *Miracle on 34ᵗʰ Street*! Remember those bags of mail, piled one on top of another, from people who confessed their belief in Santa Claus? Well, cards and letters from people who believe in the power of prayer poured into our office day after day, from all over the world: Bangkok, Buffalo, Dar es Salaam, Denver, São Paulo, Sioux Rapids, you name it. They came from teenagers and from men and women in their nineties. Hundreds and hundreds of beautiful prayers—original, traditional, short, long, perfectly typed, handwritten on the backs of napkins, or reproduced on the backs of holy cards, even prayers we had cherished as children but had forgotten and were delighted to discover anew. It wasn't as dramatic as the movie but it was, to us, much more inspiring. We asked for prayers and received a treasure chest of wisdom, gratitude, and encouragement.

We should have known.

After all, Maryknoll missioners—priests, sisters, brothers, and laity (Maryknoll Mission Association of the Faithful or MMAF)—number twelve hundred strong, and it is prayer that inspires their work with God's family, especially the poor, in forty countries on five continents. And, after all, Maryknoll supporters in the United States number almost a million, and it is prayer that sustains their faith. What else could we have expected when we asked, through *Maryknoll* magazine, for prayers from a million people dedicated to God's work?

The faith of those who responded has enriched our lives. Behind every prayer is a story of devotion, love, perseverance, and trust. The letters we received are like an inspiring mini-series of what it means to be a child of God in the world. They reveal the pain and joy of being human, the mystery and miracle of being spiritual, and the moments of grace that come to each of us, reminding us where we came from, who we are, and what we're here for.

Faith is the story behind this book.

Robert Hopkins of Ardsley, Pennsylvania, sent in "Deo Gratias," a favorite prayer of a 108–year-old woman he visited regularly as a eucharistic minister. She said all twenty-four lines from memory.

Sister Barbara Hendricks, a Maryknoller, sent in prayers and reflections of Mother Mary Joseph Rogers, the foundress of the Maryknoll Sisters.

From Lenara Tauchmann Boyd of Gordon, Texas, age 87, came a prayer she learned from her grandparents who emigrated from Germany in the 1840s.

A favorite of Barbara Hussey Riggins of Walnut Creek, California, is a prayer for peace of Marcos Garcia Diego, a 10-year-old boy from Mexico.

We drew near to these many friends of Maryknoll by reading letters aloud to each other—some absolutely had to be shared—and by praying at our daily mass for those people who requested *our* prayers.

The prayers in this book can lead us to meditation or contemplation or action, but they don't have to. It is enough that they enable us to express joy, praise, love, forgiveness, gratitude, a desire to serve, beauty, goodness, peace, harmony, trust, and other spiritual values. That is what we are here for.

The chapters in *A Maryknoll Book of Prayer* named themselves. Instead of forcing the prayers into a predetermined pattern, we let the prayers tell us where they wanted to be. For instance, many prayers expressed awe at the wonder of God's presence or spoke eloquently of the family of God or about serving God and our neighbor, and so we grouped them that way.

Our only regret is that we couldn't use all the prayers that came in. We had enough for three books, so we had to make choices. We also received multiple submissions of many favorites: more than a dozen people sent in the prayer of Father Mychal Judge, chaplain of the Fire Department of New York who was killed on September 11, 2001, and twenty friends of Maryknoll sent in the same favorite prayer of Thomas Merton. For the sake of space we have identified only the first person whose contribution we received. Every single person who contributed a prayer, however, will receive a copy of the book. And, in some cases, the original author of the prayer was not apparent. We apologize for any inadvertent errors we have made in the attributions.

This is *A Maryknoll Book of Prayer*. It reflects the church and is a mirror image of Maryknoll. Just as the Benedictines are known for their rule, the Jesuits for their learning, and the Franciscans for their simplicity, Maryknollers are known for their recognition that "whatever you do to the least of these, you do unto me." And they endeavor to remain faithful to this gospel in every corner of the earth.

All prayer traditions, of course, share basic characteristics, such as adoration and thanksgiving, and *A Maryknoll Book of Prayer* offers samplings from many different traditions. May the thoughts and prayers in this book—whether from Buddhists in Thailand or Catholics in North America or the Maasai in East Africa—help us to realize that nothing can separate us from the love of God or from each other. What knowledge could be more beautiful?

More than ever we are grateful to be part of the Maryknoll family—and to share these prayers with you.

—Michael Leach and Susan Perry
Feast of the Epiphany 2003

God with Us

In God we live and move and have our being.
ACTS 17:28

For I am persuaded, that neither death, nor life, nor angels, nor principalities, nor powers, nor things present, nor things to come, nor height, nor depth, nor any other creature, shall be able to separate us from the love of God, which is in Christ Jesus our Lord.
ROMANS 8:38–39

God is closer to us than breathing, nearer than hands and feet. Wherever we are, God is. The beginning of prayer is to know simply that—that God is with us, no matter what. God is love, and we live and move and have our being in *love*. What could be more beautiful, more consoling or more encouraging!

God is with us. Let us pray.

I am not alone
for God is always with me.
I am not afraid
for God is protecting me.
I am forgiven everything
for God is loving me.
I am bearing fruit
for God is supporting me.
I will persevere
for God is sustaining me.
I am being saved
for God is calling me.

Rose O'Brien, New Britain, Connecticut,
a friend of Maryknoll

Be Silent, Be Still

Alone, empty before your God,
say nothing, ask nothing.
Let your God look upon you;
that is all.
God knows and understands,
God loves you
with an enormous love,
waiting only to look
upon you with love.
Quiet-still-be.
Let your God love you.

Mary E. Maney, R.D.C., White Plains, New York,
a friend of Maryknoll,
from a prayer by Edwina Gateley

The light of God surrounds us.
The love of God enfolds us.
The power of God protects us.
The presence of God watches over us.
Wherever we are, God is,
and all is well.

Mary DeLong, Woodstock, New York,
a friend of Maryknoll

Prayer for the Journey

Lord, I thank you,
you have looked into my heart,
you have laid your hand upon me;
and have set a road before me;
you have called me, "Come apart."

Lord, I pray you,
that I see all with your eyes,
that you take me by the hand
on the road to other lands,
one with you for all my days.

Father John Halbert, M.M., Maryknoll, New York

"Genuine spirituality is a prayerful life rather than the completing of a certain number of spiritual exercises every day. Our whole life should be a prayer."

& *Father Joseph Healey, M.M., Dar es Salaam, Tanzania,* A Fifth Gospel *(Orbis Books, 1981)*

The road of life may take us
where we do not care to go—
Up rocky paths, down darkened trails,
our steps unsure and slow.
But the Lord of all extends
His hand to hold, to help, to guide us.
We never have to feel alone
for God walks close beside us.

Kathy Steinbock, Omaha, Nebraska,
a friend of Maryknoll,
from a prayer card
of the Norbertine Fathers

Oh, the Love of the Lord
Is the Essence

Oh, the love of my Lord is the essence of all that I love
     here on earth;
All the beauty I see He has given to me;
and His giving is gentle as silence.
Every day, every hour, every moment has been blessed by
     the strength of His love.
At the turn of each tide, He is there at my side.
And His touch is gentle as silence.
There've been times when I've turned from His presence,
and I've walked other paths, other ways.
But I've called on His name in the dark of my shame.
And His mercy was gentle as silence.

Christopher Konrad,
a missionary volunteer pharmacist
at the North Kinangop Catholic Hospital, Kenya,
a prayer/poem by an unknown author on the wall
at St. Paul University Chapel, Nairobi

O Great Spirit
whose voice I hear in the winds,
And whose breath gives life to all the world,
hear me! I am small and weak;
I need your strength and wisdom.

Let me walk in beauty, and make my eyes
ever behold the red and purple sunset.

Make my hands respect the things you have made
and my ears sharp to hear your voice.

Make me wise so that I may understand
the things you have taught my people.

Let me learn the lessons
you have hidden in every leaf and rock.

I seek strength, not to be greater than my brother,
but to fight my greatest enemy—myself.

Make me always ready to come to you
with clean hands and straight eyes.

So when life fades, as the fading sunset,
my spirit may come to you without shame.

Barbara Hussey Riggins, Walnut Creek, California,
a friend of Maryknoll, from a Lakota prayer

Lord, help me to spread thy fragrance everywhere. Flood my soul with thy Spirit and light. Shine through me and be so in me that everyone I come in contact with may feel thy presence in my soul. Let them see no longer me but only Jesus. Amen.

Bea Waltz, Chicago, Illinois,
a friend of Maryknoll, author unknown

O Mother Earth,
Soil of my birthing,

When did I stop reverencing
Your wonders
And lose sight of your
Awesome beauty?

When did I stop living
Your timeless seasons
And tasting your cool,
Refreshing water?

When did I stop climbing trees
And rolling in your
Lush meadows?

When did I stop seeing
Your stars
And feeling the soft
Embrace of your breeze?

O Mother Earth,
My Mother Earth,
Soil of my birthing,
Forgive me.

Sister Adelina St. Hilaire, Latham, New York,
from a prayer by Mary Ellen Putnam, C.S.J.

"God has created us to love and to be loved, and this is the beginning of prayer—to know that he loves me, that I have been created for greater things."

❧ *Mother Teresa*

Architect of all creation, we Your creatures sing Your praise.
From the realm of life eternal You have fashioned finite ways.
Pale reflection of Your radiance You impart to sun and star.
From the remnants of Your Being worlds emerge and so we are.

We are drops of living water, we are branches of the Vine.
We are bread and body broken, we are chalice for the Wine.
Christ incarnate, we perceive You in Your manifold disguise
and are strengthened in our dyings, knowing we will also rise.

Like the life force of our future or the stillness in a storm,
Holy Spirit, You are essence of all moments that transform.
When we taste the milk and honey, or the myrrh that makes us whole,
we say yes to Your indwelling and find solace for the soul.

God of all the generations and foundations come and gone,
in Your love we're everlasting and we will continue on.
When we seek You, we will find You in those regions where You dwell,
touch the wingtips of Your glory, and know more than we can tell.

Miriam Therese Winter, Thailand,
from The Singer and the Song
(Orbis Books, 1999)

Come, Holy Spirit, Light of the soul, that we may see in all creatures the glowing beauty of God's love.

Bishop Francis X. Ford, M.M., Kaying, China,
from Come, Holy Ghost
(Maryknoll Publications, 1953)

Earthly Harmony

Lord, the land, water and
Plants are basic to our existence.
They mean the survival of
Generations. Grant that we may
Ever co-exist in harmony with the
Mountains and the rivers, our
Source of hope. May we continue
To use them for our good, as we
Have since time immemorial. We
Are saddened by those who
Unclothe our mountains and carry
Away the wealth of our lands.
Grant us strength to defend our
Environment, so needed for
Existence and survival, which you
Have given us in your bounty. Amen.

Ibalot prayer from the Philippines

Everything is touched with mystery
because everything comes from your hands
or from the hand of the co-creator:
the paper on which I write,
the pen I use,
the table at which I find myself,

the books which surround me,
the clothes I wear,
the air I breathe,
the light I see by,
the floor which supports me. . . .

The heart trembles with happiness,
And the clear impression of being
Totally integrated in you.

Translated by Father Jerry Wickenhauser, M.M.,
São Paulo, Brazil, from one of the last prayers
written by Dom Helder Câmara of Recife, Brazil

Great Spirit,
Whose voice
I hear in the wind;
Whose breath gives
Life to the world,
Hear me.

I come to you as one of
Your many children.
I am small and weak;
I need your strength and wisdom.
May I walk in beauty.

Ellie Hays, Maryknoll Affiliate, Sparks, Nevada

Live in such a way that those who know you,
but don't know God,
will come to know God because they know you!

Louise Pranzini, San Jose, California,
a friend of Maryknoll, anonymous

Dear Lord,
I thank you for this day of life,
for feet to walk amidst the trees,
for hands to pick the flowers from the earth,
for sense of smell to breathe in the sweet perfume of nature,
for a mind to think about and appreciate the magic of
        everyday miracles,
for a spirit to swell in joy.

Rodna Walls Taylor, Oakland, California,
a friend of Maryknoll

Now, talking God,
With your feet I walk.

I walk with your limbs;
I carry forth your body.

For me your mind thinks;
Your voice speaks for me.

Beauty is before me
And beauty is behind me.

Above and below me hovers the beautiful.
I am surrounded by it;
I am immersed in it.

In my youth I am aware of it
And in old age I shall walk quietly
The beautiful trail.

Sister Elizabeth Lee, M.M., Gallup, New Mexico,
from a Native American prayer

Grandfather, Great Spirit
All over the world the faces of living ones are alike.
With tenderness they have come up out of the ground.

Look upon your children
that they may face the winds and walk the good road
to the Day of Quiet.

Grandfather, Great Spirit,
Fill us with the Light.
Give us the strength to understand
And the eyes to see.

Teach us to walk the soft Earth
as relatives to all that live.

Sister Elizabeth Lee, M.M., Gallup, New Mexico,
from a Sioux prayer

To be near God is my delight;
To be with God is my destiny;
To love God is my perfection;
To be loved by God in return
Is a gift beyond measure!

Paul Schoemann, Elma, New York,
a friend of Maryknoll,
a prayer of a Dominican friar

"The more we throw ourselves out to others, and
to others in God, the closer we draw to God, and
the more fully will our souls be nourished by the
Body of Christ."

❧ *Bishop James A. Walsh, M.M.,*
co-founder of the Maryknoll Society

Jesus, as a mother you gather your people to you;
you are gentle with us as a mother with her children.
Often you weep over our sins and our pride:
tenderly you draw us from hatred and judgment.
You comfort us in sorrow and bind up our wounds;
in sickness you nurse us,
and with pure milk you feed us.

Jesus, by your dying we are born to new life;
by your anguish and labor we come forth in joy.
Despair turns to hope through your sweet goodness;
through your gentleness we find comfort in fear.
Your warmth gives life to the dead;
your touch makes sinners righteous.

Lord Jesus, in your mercy heal us;
in your love and tenderness remake us.
In your compassion bring grace and forgiveness;
for the beauty of heaven may your love prepare us.

St. Anselm (1033–1109)

Jesus, My Jesus . . .

How marvelous are your ways.
Far more splendid than my mind can envision.
What an honor to be chosen by you.
A lowly child I am, but empowered by the Holy Spirit
to fulfill the great hope to which you have called me.
I give myself totally to you, Lord.
Take my imperfect heart and make it perfect.
Peel away the hardness.
Close the doors I have opened to the temptations of this
        world.

Gently remove the roots of painful memories, sin, doubts,
    and fears.
Discard anything that separates me from you.
Lord, fill the emptiness with the light of your love
that I might be a beacon calling the lost back to you.
To love as you love,
to serve as you serve,
to heal as you heal,
to forgive as you forgive,
always mindful of my nothingness
while doing great and marvelous things
in your name and for your glory.
This I pray, Jesus, in your name. Amen.

Carmelle Machi, Frederick, Maryland,
a friend of Maryknoll

I give you this one thought to keep—
    I am with you still, I do not sleep.
I am a thousand winds that blow,
    I am the diamond glints on snow,
I am the sunlight on ripened grain,
    I am the gentle autumn rain.
When you awaken in the morning's hush,
    I am the swift, uplifting rush of quiet birds in circled
        flight.
I am the soft stars that shine at night.
    Do not think of me as gone—
I am with you still—in each new dawn.

Asa H. Stanley, Hyannis, Massachusetts,
a friend of Maryknoll,
a Native American prayer

Mary's Good-bye Song

Go forth in peace
Don't fear the darkness
Your life and ours
Are one in the Lord.
Though you don't know this road
He walks before you
And waits ahead with open arms
To welcome you.
So lift your eyes
Set down your burden
Make your step light
And greet this day with joy.

You carried the light
And gave to all who met you
And take the same light home.
You live in our hearts
As you live in the love of the Lord.
Wherever you go
You'll never be alone.

His is the peace
That passes understanding.
His is the way
That leads beyond the dark.
Though we don't know the road
He walks beside us now
His cloak upon our shoulders
To warm us through the night.
So we leave the land
We've come to love

And follow his voice
Under the crisp new stars.

When we are weary
And cannot face the morning
He carries us safely
Within his loving arms.
Wherever we go now
We're never alone.
Wherever we go now
We're only going home.

Vicki Armour-Hileman, MMAF,
Maryknoll, New York,
on leaving Hong Kong in 1990

Receive this holy fire.
Make your lives like this fire.
A holy fire that is seen,
A life of God that is seen.
A life that has no end,
A life that darkness does not overcome.

May this light of God in you grow.
Light a fire that is worthy of your heads.
Light a fire that is worthy of your children.
Light a fire that is worthy of your fathers.
Light a fire that is worthy of your mothers.
Light a fire that is worthy of God.
Now go in peace.
May the Almighty protect you today and all days. Amen.

Father John Conway, M.M., Nairobi, Kenya,
from a Maasai prayer

Prayer of One
Who Is Moving On

Guardian, guide, no pillar of cloud by day nor fire by night,
Yet I sense your presence with me, God of the journey.
You are walking with me into a new land.
You are guarding me in my vulnerable moment.
You are dwelling with me as I depart from here.

You are promising to be my peace as I face the struggles
of distance from friends and security,
the planting of feet and heart in a strange place.

Renew in me a deep trust in you. Calm my anxiousness.
As I reflect on my life I can clearly see
how you have been there in all of my leavings.
You have been there in all of my comings.
You will always be with me in everything.
I do not know how I am being resettled,
but I place my life into the welcoming arms of your love.

Encircle my heart with your peace.
May your powerful presence run like a strong thread
through the fibers of my being. Amen.

Sharon Raynor, MMAF (Venezuela),
Maryknoll, New York,
a prayer by Joyce Rupp
from Praying Our Goodbyes
(Ave Maria Press, 1988)

Grandfather, help us to see
that what we see, what we touch
is sacred, is holy;
that the ground upon which we walk
is holy.

Help us to imitate the sun
in warming our brothers and our sisters
the birds and the trees
whose secret is peace.

Help us to be like the spring wind
which does not destroy what it touches.
This we ask through Christ our Lord. Amen.

Sister Elizabeth Lee, M.M., Gallup, New Mexico,
from Black Elk's Prayer on Mt. Harney
in the Black Hills of South Dakota

Let nothing trouble you;
Let nothing frighten you.
Everything passes.
God never changes.
Patience obtains all.
Whoever has God wants for nothing.
God alone is enough.

Agnes Sande, Las Vegas, Nevada,
a friend of Maryknoll,
a prayer of St. Teresa of Avila

Family of God

"I give you a new commandment, that you love one another. . . . By this everyone will know that you are my disciples, if you have love for one another."

JOHN 13:34–35

The body is a unit, though it is made up of many parts. . . . If one part suffers, every part suffers with it; if one part is honored, every part rejoices with it. Now you are the body of Christ, and each one of you is a part of it.

1 CORINTHIANS 12:12, 26-27

Nothing can separate us from the love of God, and nothing can separate us from each other. We are made in the image and likeness of God.

Prayer begins with the awesome recognition of our oneness with God. It continues with the realization of our unity with one another. We are all members of one family—the family of God.

Let us pray.

∾

God made us a family
We need one another
We love one another
We forgive one another
We work together
We play together
We worship together
Together we use God's word
Together we grow in Christ
Together we love all people
Together we serve our God
Together we hope for heaven
These are our hopes and ideals.
Help us to attain them, O God,
Through Jesus Christ our Lord.

Florence Sossong, Pittsburgh, Pennsylvania,
a friend of Maryknoll

We pray for the sick and suffering, the poor and the needy, the mistreated and abused, especially the little children, those without hope and those who have no one to pray for them. We ask your blessings on the helpless, especially the unborn, the unjustly imprisoned, battered women, and all those sold into slavery and prostitution.

We pray also for the priests, sisters, missioners, and all those who assist the poor.

Gene Rosenthal, Griffin, Georgia,
a friend of Maryknoll

All God's Children

We come in many shapes and sizes
And different colors too.
Our languages are many,
Our cultures quite a few.
But for all our variations
There's one thing we all share:
We're molded in His image
And protected in His care.
A Father to all children,
His arms are open wide
To welcome every one of us.
He is always by our side.
And when our troubles daunt us,
On His loving grace we call,
For whatever color, race or creed,
Our Lord God loves us all. Amen.

Bea Raiker, a friend of Maryknoll,
a prayer from Vacation Bible School
at Our Lady of Mt. Carmel

"To be a missionary . . . means that a person must be selfless, with one outstanding idea—to carry on the work that Christ has given us, under any circumstances, no matter how difficult."

◆ *Mother Mary Joseph Rogers,*
foundress of the Maryknoll Sisters

Prayer for Families

God, our Father, loving and merciful, bring together and keep all families in perfect unity of love and mutual support. Infuse in each member the spirit of understanding, forbearance, and affection for each other.

Keep quarrels, bitterness, and pettiness far from them, and for their occasional failures instill forgiveness and peace.

May the mutual love and affection of parents be a source of loving obedience and discipline. May their chastity and fidelity be an inspiration to their children.

Instill in children such self-respect that they may respect others, obey their parents and those in authority, and grow in mature independence and the tender joys of friendship.

Make the mutual affection and respect of families a sign of Christian life here and hereafter, through Jesus Christ, our Lord and Savior. Amen.

Anne and Gerald Porteus, Bedford, New York,
friends of Maryknoll

Prayer for My Family

Dear God, our loving and merciful Father, bring together and keep my family in perfect unity of love and mutual support.

Keep quarrels, bitterness, and pettiness far from us, and give us grace for forgiveness and peace.

May we find true unity through faith in you. Amen.

Julia Rispoli, Mayfield Heights, Ohio,
a friend of Maryknoll

Prayer for Families

Lord, watch over and protect my family.
Keep us safe from all harm to body and soul,
whether we stay at home or travel.
Lord, support us with your grace at all times.
Help us to be patient and kind,
understanding and forgiving at all times.
Make us mindful of your presence and your great love for
    each of us.
Jesus, Mary, and Joseph, bless my family and keep us close
    to you forever. Amen.

Phyllis Moran, Troy, Michigan,
a friend of Maryknoll

A Prayer for Spouses

Lord Jesus, grant that I and my spouse may have a true
and understanding love for each other. Grant that we may
both be filled with faith and trust. Give us the grace to live
with each other in peace and harmony. May we always
bear with one another's weaknesses and grow from each
other's strengths. Help us to forgive one another's failings and grant us patience, kindness, cheerfulness, and the
spirit of placing the well-being of the other ahead of self.

May the love that brought us together grow and mature with each passing year. Bring us both ever closer to
you through our love for each other. Let our love grow to
perfection. Amen.

Tom Sloggett, Mount Pleasant, South Carolina,
a friend of Maryknoll

A Mother's Prayer

How soft and beautiful are your little hands.
How innocently they snuggle up against my breast.
Some day . . .
Some far-off day these precious little hands must leave
        behind
the warmth, the toys of fun-filled childhood days
to find their place in the world . . .
to take up the work of mankind.

Oh, how I long to know these hands will find their place!
That some day they will make their imprint on the world.
That they will be hands used not to hurt,
nor to take from others, nor cause dishonor.
But instead will be virtuous hands—
hands to heal, or to defend, to build, to create,
to pray, to worship, to love.
Hands, that though they may become scarred
and worn from work
will have lost none of the tenderness and innocence
I see in them now.

It may be that these hands will never become famous,
but I pray that the world will be better because of their
        touch.

David A. Tomko,
Butler, Pennsylvania,
a friend of Maryknoll

Dear God, for all the children that are abused, touch them with your gentleness, let them feel your love and embrace, let them know you care. Bring them joy and not fear; bring them hope and not despair; bring them loving fathers and loving mothers; heal their pain; and heal their hearts, and let them know that you are there, always at their side, to hold them in your love. Amen.

Sister Pauline Sticka, M.M., Kaohsiung, Taiwan

Holy angels, you know I no longer guide, guard, and direct my children as when they were younger. So I entrust them to your care. I beg you, with the heart of a parent, to protect my children this day in body and soul. Strengthen their will that they may avoid evil. You see the face of the heavenly Father; ask him to lead my children along life's way to goodness, so that someday, together with you, our whole family may sing his praises in heaven. Amen.

Margaret C. Flach, Richland, Michigan,
a friend of Maryknoll

"The experience of prayer can have a remarkable impact upon relationships between people, as well as on the growth of friendship and intimacy. To be able to share the mystical dimension with another is a profound experience. . . . This deep intimacy nourishes and supports our ability to reach out to others."

✒ *Father Joseph Healey, M.M., Tanzania,*
A Fifth Gospel *(Orbis Books, 1981)*

A Prayer for Homeless Children

Dear Lord, help all boys and girls without a home of their own this day. Guide them to a place where they will feel loved and wanted, cared for and appreciated.

Lift them up when they are down. Dry their tears when they cry. Heal them when they are hurt. Should they fall, pick them up and hold them close to your heart.

Lord, you began life homeless. Mary and Joseph protected you on the journey into Egypt. Grant that today's homeless children find such loving and faithful protectors.

Bless, too, O Lord, those who care for these homeless little ones in your name. Amen.

Philip Mesisca, Stratford, New Jersey,
a friend of Maryknoll,
a prayer card from Mercy Boys' Home, Chicago

Youth

O God of all youth, we pray
To you. We are young and want
To celebrate life. We cry out
Against all that kills life. Hunger,
Poverty, unemployment,
Sickness, repression, injustice.
We announce the fullness of life,
Work, education, health, housing,
And bread for all. We want
Communion. A world renewed.
With the Lord of history. We
Want to make all things new.

Brazilian Youth

Lord Jesus Christ,
Son of the Living God,
Comforter of widows,
Washer of feet,
show us how to care for each other.
Teach us to love as you did:
Unconditionally, unilaterally,
without fear or favor,
pride, or prejudice.
Give us open hearts
and wise minds
and hands that are worthy
to serve in your name.

Sheila Cassidy, England,
from Good Friday People
(Orbis Books, 1995)

Dear Lord,
I pray for all those who are dearer to me than myself
and for them I offer up one prayer—
the prayer of the good thief on the cross.
Remember, Lord, to bless them, to console them, and to
      save them.
Remember them in the hour of temptation,
in their difficulties and their desires.
Remember them and me, above all, at the hour of death.

Leona McCall, Gloucester City, New Jersey,
a friend of Maryknoll,
a prayer she has been saying
for seventy-five years

A Daily Prayer

O Lord, open my eyes that I may see the need of others.
Open my ears that I may hear their cries.
Open my heart so that they need not be without nourish-
       ment and hope.
Let me not be afraid to defend the weak because of the
       anger of the strong,
nor to defend the poor because of the rich.
Show me where love and hope and faith are needed,
and use me to bring them to your people.
Open my eyes and ears that I may this coming day be able
       to do your work
for peace and justice wherever that may take me.

Cecelia Tucker, St. Paul, Minnesota,
a friend of Maryknoll

A Prayer of Strength in Weakness

We do not ask that You return our sight,
   but we do ask that You open the eyes
   of our society in order to discover
   the true values of justice, love, and peace.

We do not ask that You give us back our
   legs, but we do ask that our brothers and sisters
   walk united toward You.

We do not ask that You restore our hands,
   but we do ask that You teach all
   that there is more joy in giving than in
   receiving, and that fraternity is sharing
   all, as You have done with us.

We do not ask that You raise us from our
 beds, but we do ask that You give us
 the strength to touch the hearts of
 those who have given up,
 who do not believe in the light. Amen.

Sister Pat Lowery, M.M.,
Lima, Peru, from a prayer
of handicapped Peruvians

Prayer for Others

Lord, our heavenly father, you hear us praying. You hear
our brothers and sisters praying in Africa, Asia, Australia,
and in America, in Europe, and in Latin America.

We are all one in prayer and praise. We honor you and
we beg you that we may rightly carry commission to witness and to love in our church and throughout the whole
world.

We ask you to accept our prayers graciously, even when
they sound strange or confused. We ask for our own needs
and those of our brothers and sisters and depend on your
understanding to guide and open our hearts to unity in
Jesus Christ our Lord. Amen.

Lucille Koda, Stamford, Connecticut,
a friend of Maryknoll,
from an old Maryknoll prayer booklet

Prayer for a New Society

All-nourishing God, your children cry for help
Against the violence of our world:
Where children starve for bread and feed on weapons;
Starve for vision and feed on drugs;
Starve for love and feed on videos;
Starve for peace and die murdered in our streets.

Creator God, timeless preserver of resources,
Forgive us for the gifts that we have wasted.
Renew for us what seems beyond redemption;
Call order and beauty to emerge again from chaos.
Convert our destructive power into creative service;
Help us to heal the woundedness of our world.

Liberating God, release us from the demons of violence.
Free us today from the disguised demon of deterrence
That puts guns by our pillows and missiles in our skies.

Free us from all demons that blind and blunt our spirits;
Cleanse us from all justifications for violence and war;
Open our narrowed hearts to the suffering and the poor.

Abiding God, loving renewer of the human spirit,
Unfold our violent fists into peaceful hands:
Stretch our sense of family to include our neighbors;
Stretch our sense of neighbor to include our enemies
Until our response to you finally respects and embraces
All creation as precious sacraments of your presence.

Hear the prayer of all your starving children. Amen.

Father Leo Shea, M.M., Maryknoll, New York,
a prayer from Pax Christi USA

Lord, when I am hungry,
   Give me someone in need of food;
When I am cold,
   Give me someone to warm;
When I have no time,
   Give me someone I can help for a little while;
When I am in need of understanding,
      Offer me someone to console.

Lisa Jo Looney, MMAF alumna,
Mwanza, Tanzania

Lord of all our troubled world:
We pray for all who suffer,
for refugees and orphans,
for families disrupted by war.
We pray for church workers and missionaries,
for all who work with the afflicted.
Help us to work for justice,
without which we have no right to peace.

Sheila Cassidy, England,
from Good Friday People
(Orbis Books, 1995)

"The true proficiency of the soul consists not in
much thinking but in much loving."
ᴥ *Bishop James A. Walsh, M.M.,*
co-founder of the Maryknoll Society

Lord, I speak to you with gratitude. On every side I see the abundant blessings you have given to our country. Even though we face sorrow and sufferings, our burdens are light compared to our brothers and sisters in the human family. Increase in us, Lord, the gift of faith so that we might see all people as your sons and daughters. Don't let us be blind to our fellowship in Christ because of the different colors of our skin. Don't let us be dead to your command of love because of our different political systems. Don't let us become isolated in fear of one another because of race or creed or difference of age.

Help those whom you have blessed so abundantly to reach out and touch with generosity the lives of the poor. Give us the courage to help our mighty nation to use its power to bring freedom and dignity to all peoples. Help each of us, whoever or wherever we are, to realize that our lives may be the only gospel that our neighbor may ever read. Amen.

Lucille Koda, Stamford, Connecticut,
a friend of Maryknoll,
from an old Maryknoll prayer booklet

Prayer for Missioners

God, help me to cross human-made borders
to stand with all your sons and daughters
who live on the edge.
May everything I say and do help them realize
how much you love, forgive, and care for them.

Father Joseph Veneroso, M.M.,
Maryknoll, New York

A Better World

God, our Father, so many men and women of our world
      are hungry and destitute.
So many children die in poverty and neglect.
And so many more don't know what to do with their riches.
It's unfair, Lord!

So many men and women of our world are victims of
      brutality and war.
So many children lose their parents, so many parents lose
      their children!
Close to us, children are abandoned.
Close to us, men and women are homeless and cast out.
Sometimes, Lord, this world does not seem very good.

Come, Lord, and help us build a better world where peace
      replaces war,
where there is understanding and no violence, love and no
      selfishness.
Show us, Lord Jesus, what to do to change the world.
Open our eyes, our hearts and our hands so that we may
      take in those who need us.
Don't let us pass them by with indifference.
Lord, in the small world of our family,
give us the strength to treat each other with care, respect
      and kindness. Amen.

Regina Barcewicz, Troy, Michigan,
a friend of Maryknoll,
a prayer from a Capuchin Retreat Center

Our Father of the Poor

Our Father:
of each one of us: of the poor, of the elderly, of the needy, of those who seek justice, of all true Christians;

Who art in heaven:
and also in the poorest of places, and in our meetings, and in the communities; but also in the prisons where there are tortures, and also in those places where they search for justice for the poor, where there are persecutions, where there are undernourished children, and where God is celebrated;

Hallowed be Thy name:
But really! We look for your kingdom on earth and in heaven. We accept your programs, your news for the poor; liberty for the poor and freedom for those who announce your name.

Thy will be done on earth as it is in heaven:
which is not the case today. Rather, there is killing among brothers and sisters; rejection of those who seek justice; rejection of religious; rejection of the poor; of the prophets; rejection of those who announce the true word of God; rejection of truth, of union, of equality for our poor brothers and sisters.

Give us this day our daily bread:
which we need for our destitute brothers and sisters. A daily bread that will also be the fulfillment of your kingdom begun here on earth and finished in heaven; your kingdom for all of our brothers and sisters.

Forgive us our trespasses as we forgive those who trespass against us:

on so many occasions and in so many ways: the destruction of an organized community, the destruction of the church of the poor. Don't let your children be mistreated, and free us from all evil thinking.

And deliver us from evil:
which looks to dominate the poor who suffer violence in Nicaragua, El Salvador, Guatemala, and in our own countries.

We pray that those hearts of those brothers and sisters of ours, which seem to be of stone, may be converted to hearts of flesh, and that they may be with the Holy Spirit, and that the Lord will enlighten them. Amen.

Community of C'uchu Pupuja,
Santiago de Pupuja, Puno, Peru

Dear Lord, we thank you for the privilege of associating with your children, the Mayan Indians. We see their stamina and courage in hardships. We admire their quiet dignity and humbleness. We learn of the precious quality of embracing each other's needs, and their love of the church. We pray that they set a good example for us. Father, forgive our sins against the unity of your family and make us one in heart and spirit. Amen.

Peggy Santos, San Diego, California,
a Maryknoll Affiliate,
a prayer of Phyllis Armstrong,
a companion to Guatemalan migrant workers

Let the Third World Peoples Speak

I believe in God the Parent of us all, who
    Has given the earth to all people.
I believe in Jesus Christ, who came
    to encourage us and to heal us,
    to deliver us from oppressors,
    to proclaim the peace of God to all.
    He has given himself to the world;
    The Lord lives among ALL people; he is
    among us as the living God.
I believe in God's spirit, who works in
    Every man and woman of good will.
I believe in the Church, called to be a
    light for all nations, urged by the Spirit
    to serve ALL people.
I believe that God will finally destroy the
    power of sin in all of us, and that all will
    share God's everlasting life.

I do NOT believe in the right of the strongest,
    nor the force of arms,
    nor the power of oppressors.
I want to believe in human rights,
    in the solidarity of ALL people,
    in the power of nonviolence.

I do NOT believe in racism, in wealth,
    privilege, or the established order.
I want to believe that all women and men are
    equal; and that order based on violence
    and injustice is NOT order.

I do NOT believe we can ignore things which
    happen far away.
I want to believe that the whole world is my
    home, and that the field that I plough and
    the harvest I reap belong to everyone.

I do NOT believe that I can fight oppression
    far away, if I tolerate injustice here.
I want to believe that there is but one
    right everywhere; that I am not free
    if even one person remains enslaved.

I do NOT believe that war and hunger are
    inevitable, and peace unattainable.
I want to believe in the beauty of simplicity,
    in love with open hands,
    in genuine peace on earth—in our time.

I do NOT believe that all suffering is in vain,
    nor that our dreams will remain but
    dreams, nor that death is the end.

But I DARE to believe,
    always and in spite of everything,
    in a new humanity; in God's own dream of
    a new heaven which is a new earth where
    genuine peace will flourish because there
    is JUSTICE.

Father Tom Marti, M.M.,
Maryknoll, New York,
from an Indonesian creed

Andean Credo

The first Andean Congress of Christian base communities was held in October 1986 in Oruro, Bolivia. Participants wrote the following creed to summarize their hopes for the growing movement of small Christian communities:

We believe in God, the all-powerful creator, who gives us life, who desires justice and equality, who loves the poor with a preferential love, who brings together a people, who desires change and who journeys with us in the search for the promised land.

We believe in Jesus, our brother, God's word incarnate in a humble and suffering people carrying the cross of oppression.

We believe that those who have the last word are not the Pontius Pilates or the oppressors of this world but the people who go forth celebrating the resurrection—the victory of the God of life.

We believe in the Spirit of Jesus who acts through this people's poverty, powerlessness, ignorance, weakness, suffering and persecution in order to build a world of solidarity, justice and love.

We believe in the Spirit, who is present and guides Christian base communities, seeds of the reign that are building a new model of church—the community of Jesus: prophetic, missionary, liberating and committed to the people.

We believe in the power of the Spirit who gives us hope to destroy the monster of injustice and hunger that prevails in Latin America.

We believe in Christian base communities, guided by Mary, humble woman of the people and the model of a new relationship between men and women. In them we, the poor, are authors of our own liberation.

Sister Rosemary McCormack, M.M., Lima, Peru,
from Latinamerica Press, *1987*

Shine On, Farmer Boy

Shine on, farmer boy, symbol to me of the thousand million like you who drew the Son of God from heaven to smooth and bless your weary anxieties and your puzzled brows. Come to me often in your barefoot squalor and look at me from out of those hopeless and bewildered eyes. Do not let me forget that vision, but stay by me and preside over my dreams. Teach me that souls are people. And remind me everlastingly that they are magnificent people like you.

A prayer of Bishop James E. Walsh, M.M.,
for the people of China

"I feel that the reason we seem to come closer to one another is because we have come closer to God."

❦ *Bishop James A. Walsh, M.M.,*
co-founder of the Maryknoll Society

Children's Creed

I believe in God, Father and Mother, creator of children
     on earth.
I believe in Jesus Christ, son and child of God,
    Like all children, one in being with the Parents.
    To him all children came.
    To bless and praise them, he was born of his mother,
    Mary, and became a child.
For the sake of the dreams and the hopes of the children
    He suffered, as many children suffer,
    He died, as many children die,
    And he rose again to be with his Parents,
    As the Spirit of the children rises within us.
He will come again to seek the children,
    And their dreams will have no end.
I believe in the Spirit
    Of joy, happiness and innocence
    That gives life to the children,
    As the Parents and Christ give them life.
With the Parents and Christ, I glorify the children.
I believe in the oneness of children.
I acknowledge that I can not enter the house of God
    Unless I am like a child.
I look to the children for the hope of the
    Life of the world to come. Amen.

Father Tom Marti, M.M., Maryknoll, New York,
written by Fred Birondo-Goddard,
inspired in 1986 while holding a child
during a liturgy in Davao City, Philippines

God of all compassion,
comfort Your sons and daughters
who live with AIDS.
Spread over us all Your quilt of mercy,
love and peace.

Open our eyes to Your presence
    reflected in their faces.
Open our ears to Your truth
    echoing in their hearts.

Give us the strength
    to weep with the grieving,
    to walk with the lonely,
    to stand with the depressed.

May our love mirror Your love
for those who live in fear,
    who live under stress and
    who suffer rejection.

Mothering, Fathering God,
grant rest to those who have died
and hope to all who live with HIV.

God of life, help us find the cure now
and help us build a world in which
no one dies alone and where
everyone lives accepted,
wanted and loved.

Father Dan Jensen, M.M., Los Altos, California,
for Maryknoll's AIDS Task Force

AIDS Way of the Cross

Opening Prayer: We adore you, O Christ, as you carry your cross along the dusty roads of Masaka, Uganda. We make the way of the cross in the homes and at the bedsides of those with AIDS. We bless you because through this suffering you have redeemed the world.

1st Station: "Jesus Is Condemned to Death." He sits shocked, unable to speak. His hands tremble. Marko has just been told he has AIDS. "I'm going to die," he says.

2nd Station: "Jesus Takes Up His Cross." He is weighed down with the knowledge that he has AIDS. How will he tell his family? What will happen to his children? He tells his brother, sells some land, arranges for his children. It's hard. It's a heavy cross Vincent carries.

3rd Station: "Jesus Falls for the First Time." He cannot stand alone. The abscesses are too painful. Peter is too weak. With help he makes it home and to bed where he begins the difficult task of regaining strength, so he can pick up the cross of living with AIDS and continue his journey.

4th Station: "Jesus Meets His Mother." She lies there waiting for her mother to return. Regina has just learned that she has AIDS and is dying. She wants to tell her mother. As they meet, a look of pain and love passes between them. "I have slim" [as AIDS is known in Africa]. Her mother takes her in her arms and they weep.

5th Station: "Simon Helps Jesus Carry His Cross." Richard has so many decisions to make. How can he go on? When his brothers come, he tells them he is too scared to go on. They comfort him, arrange to take him home, plan transport so he can return for treatment.

6ᵗʰ Station: "Veronica Wipes the Face of Jesus." She lies there, too weak to clean herself. Her clothes are dirty and soiled because the diarrhea is almost constant now. She's alone. Pushed into a corridor so the smell won't disturb others. A young nurse comes, washes her and changes her clothes. Rose smiles.

7ᵗʰ Station: "Jesus Falls the Second time." He has begun to have diarrhea and no longer wants to eat. Sleep doesn't come and he's afraid. The illness is getting worse. Peter has to stop work. It's hard to keep living with AIDS.

8ᵗʰ Station: "Jesus Meets the Women of Jerusalem." Jane has no land. Mary has no milk for her baby. Scovia's husband sent her away when he learned she has AIDS. Juliet was put out of her rented room. Betty works in a bar to support her children, providing favors for men to get food for them. The plight of poor women and AIDS. Jesus weeps.

9ᵗʰ Station: "Jesus Falls the Third Time." His head feels as if it's bursting. Nothing brings relief. Peter lies in bed unable even to open his eyes. As the end nears, relatives arrive to move him from his rented room where he suffered alone for many months. One more step along the way.

10ᵗʰ Station: "Jesus Is Stripped of His Garments." They put her out of the house and kept her clothes, saying they wouldn't fit her wasted body. They told her to go to her grandmother's to die. Once there, she was again rejected—stripped of all, even her right to belong. Juliet was returned to the hospital like an unwanted commodity.

11ᵗʰ Station: "Jesus Is Nailed to the Cross." He cannot move. Finds it hard to breathe. Must wait for someone to care for him totally. An AIDS-related brain tumor has nailed James to his bed. His mother keeps watch.

12ᵗʰ Station: "Jesus Dies on the Cross." Rose, Peter, John, Alecha, Kakande, Joseph, William, George, Grace, Paulo, Goretti . . . Jesus' body dying of AIDS.

13ᵗʰ Station: "Jesus Is Taken Down from the Cross." The wailing begins. The car reaches the homestead. As men rush forward to carry Paulo's shrouded body, a woman comes from the house. She reaches out to touch the body of her son.

14ᵗʰ Station: "Jesus Is Placed in the Tomb." A grave is dug on hospital land—only staff for mourners. Her nine-month-old child cries, not understanding. The grave is filled. All go away. Rose is dead.

15ᵗʰ Station: "The Resurrection." We wait!

Sister Kay Lawlor, M.M.M., Kitovu Hospital,
Masaka, Uganda

Proclaiming Your Resurrection

Help us, O risen Lord,
to proclaim your resurrection,
by bringing good news to the poor
and healing the hearts that are broken.

Help us, O risen Lord,
to proclaim your resurrection,

by feeding those who are hungry
and clothing those who are naked.

Help us, O risen Lord,
to proclaim your resurrection,
by releasing the captives of injustice
and all those who are imprisoned by their sins.

Help us, O risen Lord,
to proclaim your resurrection,
by welcoming the strangers
and visiting those in loneliness.

Help us, O risen Lord,
to proclaim your resurrection,
by bringing your peace to those who are in trouble
and your joy to those who are in sorrow.

God our Father,
who raised your Son from the dead,
help us to understand, we beg you,
that we conquer our own death
and rise with Jesus today
when we live in love.

We ask you this grace through Jesus Christ,
who died for our sins
and rose for our life.

Father Leo Shea, M.M., Maryknoll, New York

We bring before you, O Lord,
the troubles and perils of people and nations,
the sighing of prisoners and captives,
the sorrows of the bereaved,
the necessities of strangers,
the helplessness of the weak,
the despondency of the weary,
the failing powers of the aged.
O Lord, draw near to each;
for the sake of Jesus Christ our Lord.

St. Anselm (1033–1109)

We beg you, Lord, to help and defend us.
Deliver the oppressed,
have compassion on the despised,
raise the fallen,
reveal yourself to the needy,
heal the sick,
bring back those who have strayed from you,
feed the hungry,
lift up the weak,
remove the prisoners' chains.
May every nation come to know that you are God alone,
that Jesus is your Son,
that we are your people, the sheep of your pasture.

St. Clement of Rome (c. 30–100)

Litany of Intercession

Response: Lord, have mercy.
Leader:

For those who suffer because of the death of a loved one. R
For those who suffer because of sickness, injury, or
        disability. R
For those who suffer because of religious persecution. R
For those who suffer because of addiction. R
For those who suffer because of old age or incapacitation. R
For those who suffer because they are not understood. R
For those who suffer because of pain. R
For those who suffer because of need, hunger, or poverty. R
For those who suffer because of the tyranny of sin. R
For those who suffer because of catastrophes or natural
        disasters. R
For those who suffer because of toilsome work and degra-
        ding jobs. R
For those who suffer because of being neglected, over-
        looked, or underappreciated. R
For those who suffer because of a broken heart. R
For those who suffer because of ignorance or lack of
        education. R
For those who suffer because of bad memories, resent-
        ment, or guilt. R
For those who suffer because of mockery, ridicule, or
        humiliation. R
For those who suffer because of abuse. R
For those who suffer because of injustice or oppression. R
For those who suffer because of prejudice, discrimina-
        tion, racism, or marginalization. R
For those who suffer because of violence, cruelty, hatred,
        or war. R

For those who suffer because of homelessness, displacement, or incarceration. R
For couples who suffer because they are not able to have children. R
For those who suffer because of remorse, depression, anxiety, or mental anguish. R
For those who suffer because of rejection or abandonment. R
For those who suffer because of unemployment. R
For those who suffer because of failure. R
For those who suffer because of loneliness. R
For those who suffer because of the feeling of being worthless or unwanted. R
For parents who suffer because of the loss of a child. R
For those who suffer because of any affliction. R
For those who suffer because of betrayal. R

Margaret Ramsey, Anoka, Minnesota
a friend of Maryknoll

Dear God,
    My soul is silent with your presence in my heart.
    As I listen to the drum beat at a nearby temple,
    and the chanting of hymns of praise
    moved on by gongs and cymbals
    bringing forth the sound of prayer and worship
      of another faith
      another belief system
      another culture
      another people of this earth
      another form of worship
    searching and reaching to know your Presence.

God, I know you live and dwell in every
    human being living on this planet
    created to your image
    created by your love
    created to return to the center of the universe
    where you are.

These sounds of prayer reach into my heart and I know
        you are there—
    listening—waiting and answering
through that same mystery of life
which will take us all into your eternal embrace.

Sister Pauline Sticka, M.M., Kaohsiung, Taiwan

Voices That Challenge

Call us to hear the voices that challenge
deep in the hearts of all people
By serving your world as lovers and dreamers
We become voices that challenge
For we are the voice of God.

Voices that challenge . . . the children who long to be heard
        and respected.
Voices that challenge . . . the lowly and broken destroyed
        by oppression.
Voices that challenge . . . the old and the fearful who hope
        for a new day. . . .

Voices that challenge . . . the lives and the cries of the poor
        and the silenced.
Voices that challenge . . . the young ones who dream of a
        world free of hatred.
Voices that challenge . . . the ones who seek peace by their
        witness and courage. . . .

Voices that challenge . . . the women who suffer the pain
of injustice.
Voices that challenge . . . the prophets and heroes who
call us to question.
Voices that challenge . . . the healers who teach us forgiveness and mercy.
Voices that challenge . . . the victims of violent abuse and
aggression.
Voices that challenge . . . the Christ who gave his life that
we might live. . . .

Maryknoll Mission Association of the Faithful,
a song by Davis Haas, © 1990 GIA Publications,
used by permission

Prayer of Dom Helder Câmara

Let me now turn to God and translate in my prayer the
hope of those who are voiceless in a world that crushes them:

Father, how can we fail
to gather all humankind
into prayer,
since your Divine Son,
our brother Jesus Christ,
shed his blood
for all people,
of all lands,
of all times?

But hear, O Lord,
my special prayer
for my people,
the voiceless ones.
There are thousands

and thousands
of human creatures
in the poor countries,
and in the slums
of the rich countries,
with no right
to raise their voices,
no possibility
of claiming
of protesting,
however just
are the rights
they have to uphold.

The homeless,
the starving,
the ragged,
the wasted,
with no chance
of education,
no work,
no future,
no hope;
they may end up
believing
it was meant to be,
and losing heart,
become the silent,
the voiceless ones.

If all of us
who believe in you
had helped our rich brothers and sisters,
by opening their eyes,

stirring their consciences,
the unjust
would not have advanced,
and the gap
between rich and poor,
between individuals and groups,
between countries,
even between continents,
would not be so glaring.

Do in us, O Lord,
what we have failed
and still fail
to do.
How difficult it is
to get beyond the barrier
of aid, of gifts,
of assistance,
and reach the realm
of justice!
The privileged grow angry:
our judgment
is unfair, they say.
Meanwhile they discover
subversion
and Communism
in the most democratic,
the most human,
the most Christian gestures! Amen.

Father Tom Marti, M.M., Maryknoll, New York,
from The Voice of the Voiceless
(Orbis Books, 1985)

Dear Lord, we have felt the fear and the grief that hatred brings. Help us to bond together as your people to heal the pain, cherish the memories, and learn to celebrate our differences. You created us all as your very dear children, teach us to live in the example of your only Son, to live in faith, be confident in hope, act in charity, and believe in the power of prayer. Help us to find peace within our hearts and among all nations. Amen.

Anne Pichler, New Port Richey, Florida,
a friend of Maryknoll,
a prayer of Alice Trumbull from a prayer
card of the Association of Marian Helpers

A Daily Prayer for Justice and Mercy

Jesus, with the Father and the Holy Spirit,
Give us your compassion for those in prison.
Mend in mercy the broken in mind and memory.
Soften the hard of heart, the captives of anger.
Free the innocent; parole the trustworthy.
Awaken the repentance that restores hope.
May prisoners' families persevere in their love.

Jesus, heal the victims of crime who live with the scars.
Lift to eternal peace those who die.
Grant to victims' families the forgiveness that heals.
Give wisdom to lawmakers and to those who judge.
Instill prudence and patience in those who guard.
Make those in prison ministry bearers of your light,
for all of us are in need of your mercy. Amen.

Hilde Wendling, Port Charlotte, Florida,
a friend of Maryknoll

Prayer to the Shepherd of the Universe

Shepherd of the universe, who reconciles all peoples, gather the stray sheep and bind up wounds with your healing love. We ask you to guide and protect every member of the human family. Bring nations together in peaceful concord ensuring liberty and justice for all. Bring peoples of every race and creed to respect one another in faith, hope, and love as sons and daughters of the living God. Bring families a deep spirit of love and unity, loyalty, mutual encouragement and understanding.

Gather up all those who have strayed from your love, who are bitter and cynical, defiant and rebellious. Gather up hardened criminals and perverts, drug pushers and all those who lead others astray. Gather up all young people who have lost a sense of meaning in life, who wander aimlessly and hopelessly.

Heal the poor and the unwanted, the dejected and lonely. Heal the sick and the dying, especially those enduring extreme physical pain and permanent disabilities. Heal all mental illnesses and handicaps, the despairing, drug addicts and alcoholics.

Lord, you have told us many times that you came to be our Shepherd, to rescue us from evil and to bring us to the springs of life. We thank you for this promise, for the blood that you have poured down upon us as Lamb of God, bringing us to infinite love as you reconciled us to the Father through your Spirit, for ever and ever. Amen.

Susan Rangel, Lubbock, Texas,
a friend of Maryknoll

The Corporal Works of Mercy

1. Feed the hungry
2. Give drink to the thirsty
3. Clothe the naked
4. Visit the imprisoned
5. Shelter the homeless
6. Visit the sick
7. Bury the dead

Praise to You, Lord Jesus Christ!

I pray for the people all around us whose lives are difficult and troubled and whose suffering is unseen. For those who are in pain and cannot pray for themselves, please come to their assistance and relieve their suffering.

I pray for those who are sad and disillusioned, for the homeless and for those who can no longer find any meaning in life and may even be contemplating suicide. I also pray for people who are alone in life and who cannot get through the day or find friendship anywhere.

I pray, God, for all who are victims, murdered people, those who die in traffic accidents, for prisoners and strangers, for refugees without a country, for people who live in conflict with one another and who cannot find any solution. Please protect us from the terrorists of this world and from those who cause others to suffer. May evil never triumph over good.

I pray for children who are abused; may they be rescued from their abusers. I pray for children who have no parents and for children who are very ill and for their worried parents. Please perform some miracles.

I pray for women who are considering abortion. Please guide them to choose life for their child.

I also pray to you, God, for people with mental illness. Please release them from the prison of their mind; and for people with chemical dependencies, please give them strength to overcome them.

I pray for those who are ill without any hope of cure. For our dead, remember their names and preserve their lives into life everlasting.

Thank you, God, for each other, family, friends, and each and every moment of our lives.

Patricia Kozikowski, Sterling Heights, Michigan,
a friend of Maryknoll,
a prayer from a church bulletin
to which she has added

Joseph and Mary and Jesus, your family was remarkable for your faithfulness, your trust in God, and your care for one another. Teach us, each of us, in whatever situations our families live, to follow in your way, to be together as light for others and as tightly bound to one another, in the Word of God made flesh, as you were on earth. May we hope to share in the glory of your family, the glory of all the kingdom of God, and the glory of those who have gone before us in faith and those who will come after us. Bind us together forever in your trinitarian love. Amen.

Megan McKenna,
from Mary, Mother of All Nations
(Orbis Books, 2000)

Eyes to See

Prayer is more than words, more even than listening to "the still, small voice of God." It is also about *seeing*— seeing the God who is with us and in our neighbor and the love of God that surrounds, embraces, and fills us.

Prayer is like a sixth sense that sees the invisible. It helps us to hear love in a cry for help, and it sees and appreciates beauty, love, and peace in all that God has made.

Let us pray.

❦

Lord, our God,
Give us the eyes to see your face
the ears to know your voice
among ordinary people,
both the good and the bad.
Let us not be fooled
by the wrapping:
by dull brown paper
or tawdry ribbon,
but grant us the insight,
the patience and gentleness,
to unwrap, to uncover,
the gifts that lie hidden
in all your people.
Help us to share the pain of others,
to learn what it means to be fully human.

Sheila Cassidy, England,
from Good Friday People
(Orbis Books, 1995)

Help me, Jesus, to open my heart to the needs of those
        around me.
Let me see using your eyes.
Let me hear using your ears.
Let me love using your heart.

Celso S. Bate, Mandaluyong City, Philippines,
a friend of Maryknoll,
a prayer reflection during a visit to China

Wisdom Spirit, you who are compassionate Love
    of the Creator and Eternal Word,

Teach us, while we are on earth
    to pour out compassion and mercy
from the depth of our hearts.

When we seek and find the stranger, the broken, the
            prisoner,
    enable us to comfort them and offer them our help.

Show us how to help the poor and dedicate our
    bodies to the service of the broken.

Give us eyes to see all things in You,
    and You in all things

That we may mirror you, Most Holy Spirit,
    as we share in the Cosmic Mission of God's Reign
    and the unfolding of your Dream for all Creation. Amen.

Sister Elizabeth Lee, M.M., Gallup, New Mexico,
from a Native American prayer

God of light and life, help me to see every sunrise as a
glorious symbol of the light you send into the world. Help
me to reflect your light in ways that will help others see
the way. Fill me with your light so that there will be no
dark places in my soul. In the name of Jesus, light of the
world. Amen.

Antoinette Bossard, Roseville, Minnesota,
a friend of Maryknoll,
a prayer of Father Michael T. McEwen

Prayer of St. Teresa of Avila

Christ has no body now but yours,
No hands, no feet on earth but yours.
Yours are the eyes through which He looks compassion
  on this world;
Yours are the feet with which He walks to do good.

Yours are the hands with which He blesses all the world.
Yours are the hands, yours are the feet, yours are the eyes.
You are His body.

Christ has no body now but yours,
No hands, no feet on earth but yours.
Yours are the eyes through which He looks compassion
  on this world;
Christ has no body now on earth but yours.

Father Tom Marti, M.M., Maryknoll, New York,
from a song of John Michael Talbot

Prayer for Holiness

God, help me be truly holy.
Not so that everyone sees You in me,
but that I might see You in everyone.

Father Joseph Veneroso, M.M.,
Maryknoll, New York

The Person Next to You

The person next to you
Is the greatest miracle
And the greatest mystery
You will ever meet at this moment,
A testament of the Word made flesh.

The person next to you is an
Inexhaustible reservoir of
Possibility, with possibilities
That have only been partially
Touched off.

The person next to you is a
Unique universe of experience
Seething with necessity and
Possibility, dread and desire
Smiles and frowns, laughter and
Tears, fears and hopes,
All struggling to find expression.

The person next to you is surging
To become something in particular
To arrive at some destination
To have a story, and a song
To be known and to know.

The person next to you believes
In something, something precious,
Stands for something, counts for
Something, lives for something.

The person next to you labors
For something, waits for

Something, runs for something
Runs toward something.

The person next to you has
Problems and fears, wonders how
She is doing and often doesn't
Feel very good about it, is often
Undecided and disorganized and
Painfully close to chaos.

The person next to you
Is endowed with great toughness
In the face of adversity able to
Survive the most unbelievable
Difficulties and persecutions.

The person next to you is a
whole colony of persons, persons
Met all during his lifetime,
Really a community in which still
Lives a father and a mother,
A friend and an enemy.

The person next to you has something
She can do well, something she can do
Better than anyone else in the world,
There is something her one life on
Earth means and cares for; but does
She dare speak of it to you?

The person next to you can live
With you, not just alongside, she
Can live not only for herself
But also for you.

The person next to you can never
Be fully understood; he is more than
Any description or explanation;
He can never be fully controlled
Nor should he be.

The person next to you can comfort,
Encounter, understand, forgive you,
If that is what you want; and in turn
She is to be understood/forgiven also.

All:
The person next to you is mystery.
The word made flesh is mystery.
The word dwells among us.
So, sisters and brothers, look around you,
For God is here;
The ground on which you stand is holy.

Anonymous

Small Thing

Jesus, what you ask of us every day
    for us to bring to you
are just simple acts of love
    done in the smallest thing.

Father Michael D. Bassano, M.M.,
Bangkok, Thailand

Alone

Today I walked in the garden—alone . . .
But truly I was not alone.
I watched the birds in the trees;
I could feel the coming of the rain.
Then I hung the feeder on its chain.

The sky was a silvery gray,
Such a cool and comfortable day.
Our newly planted little trees
Quickly felt the rising breeze,
And then the rain did fall. . . .

God was there,
I was not alone.
His Holy Water,
Had set the tone.

Helen M. Higgs, Port Orchard, Washington,
a friend of Maryknoll

"The reality is that there is no better use of the time we are given in this world than to spend it in prayer in the presence of the Lord. Such prayer changes a person at his or her roots."
✦ *Father Donald McQuade, M.M., Davao City, Philippines, from* To Pray in That Secret Place *(St. Paul Publications, Philippines, 1989)*

Reflections of God

Where there is beauty,
There is God.

In a mother's face and a baby's
Smile, an old man's stories and
A laughing child. In clear blue
Skies and sparkling waters,
Birds on the wing and verdant
Flowers. There is God.

❧ *A friend of the missions*

My Prayer

God, give me eyes that I might see that work that can be
        done by me.

God, give me ears that I may hear the cries of those that
        need me near.

God, give me lips that I might speak comfort and peace to
        all who seek.

God, give me a mind that I might know to help the ones
        who need me so.

God, give me hands that I might do some large or simple
        task for you.

God, give me prayer, that I may pray for help and guid-
        ance every day.

And this thing all else above, God, give me a heart that I
        might love.

Mary Pergamo, Renton, Washington,
a friend of Maryknoll

The Body of Christ

The Lord has given us eyes to see
  The wonders He has made,
From smallest leaf to tallest tree
  His majesty displayed.

The Lord has given us ears to hear
  His message loud and clear:
If we love God and all humankind,
  His kingdom will be near.

The Lord has given us lips to speak
  His truth to all we meet.
Let us bring His peace and love
  To everyone we greet.

The Lord has given us hands to do
  His work which must be done.
Let us serve all humankind
  As taught by His own Son.

The Lord has given us feet to walk
  The path Christ walked before.
The Christian path is hard to walk,
  But it leads to heaven's door.

Catherine J. Buchta, Garwood, Texas,
a friend of Maryknoll

For Christ plays in ten thousand places,
lovely in limbs, lovely in eyes not his,
to the Father,
Through the features of [our] faces.
✒ *Gerard Manley Hopkins*

Where Can I Find My God?

I sought you, O my God, in the vast darkness of the heavens, among the millions of stars. I sought you, O God, in the brightness of the sun. I sought you, O God, in the quiet places, by babbling brooks, in the still before the dawn, in the quiet at the end of day as the sun set slowly. I thought I heard your voice in the soft summer breeze as it whispered through the pines. I thought I heard you speak in the chattering of birds and squirrels at the break of dawn. I thought I heard your whisper in the rustling of leaves. I know you are here, O God, in all these things.

But truly, you cannot touch me through them. Only hands such as you have created can touch another human being, only hands, only love can touch our hearts. Your love, and the love of those that you gave us on earth, this is truly where we will find you. In the face of a smiling child, or an elderly loved one, in the touch of a hand from someone we love and cherish dear, a touch, a smile, the warm glow that comes from knowing that we are loved.

These are the gifts you give us to show us you care and you are here with us, and we are loved. Where can I find my God? I open my eyes and look around, and see him every day in the faces of those he loves; the light in their eyes is his light, the love in their hearts is his love, the touch of their hand is his touch.

With so many reminders around me very day, how can I not see my God!

Robert Rainer, Grand Rapids, Michigan,
a friend of Maryknoll

God our Father, you who tell us
that your love fills the earth
and that your tenderness is for each person
that of a father for his children,
   we pray to you:

Make your light shine in our hearts
so that we can recognize
that your Word is true,
and that your love rests upon each of us
when you give us your only Son, Jesus Christ.

Give us the grace, Lord,
to look for you in the love of our brothers and sisters,
to discover your name in their faces,
to meet you in the heart of our life,
and to reveal to all people
that you wish to fill them with your joy and peace. Amen.

A prayer from Maryknoll
based on Psalm 103:13

Give us a pure heart
That we may see thee,
A humble heart,
That we may hear thee,
A heart of love
That we may serve thee,
A heart of faith
That we may live thee.

Dag Hammarskjöld

The light of God surrounds me,
The love of God enfolds me,
The power of God protects me,
The presence of God watches over me.
Where I am, God is.

Hilde Wendling, Port Charlotte, Florida,
a friend of Maryknoll, author unknown

Dedication to Service

"I was hungry and you gave me something to eat, I was thirsty and you gave me something to drink, I was a stranger and you invited me in, I needed clothes and you clothed me, I was sick and you looked after me, I was in prison and you came to visit me. . . . I tell you the truth, whatever you did for one of the least of these brothers or sisters of mine, you did for me."

MATTHEW 25:34–36, 40

Prayer inspires us not only to see the Christ in everyone, but to *be* the Christ to everyone. We begin to understand: the hungry child in India is our sister; the man dying of AIDS in Africa is our brother. The woman on welfare, the soccer mom, the businessman, the teenage volunteer—all of us are somehow mysteriously *one*.

We know then that what happens to the least of them—both the good and the bad—happens to all of us.

Let us pray.

❧

Lord, take me where you want me to go.
Let me meet whom you want me to meet.
Tell me what you want me to say.
And keep me out of your way.

Father Frank Diffley, M.M.,
Maryknoll, New York,
from a prayer of
Father Mychal Judge, Chaplain, FDNY

O God, who would have all people be saved and come to a knowledge of the Truth, send forth, we beseech you, laborers into your harvest, and grant them with all boldness to preach the word, that your gospel may everywhere be heard and glorified, and him whom you have sent, Jesus Christ your Son, our Lord. Amen.

Sister Barbara Hendricks, M.M.,
Maryknoll, New York,
from a prayer for vocations
of Mother Mary Joseph Rogers,
foundress of the Maryknoll Sisters

Bishop Ford's Prayer

Grant us, Lord, to be the doorstep by which the multitudes may come to worship Thee. And if, in the saving of their souls, we are ground underfoot and spat upon and worn out, at least we shall have served Thee in some small way in helping pagan souls; we shall have become the King's highway to their salvation. Amen.

Maryknoll Fathers' Prayer Book, *1963*

A Vocation Blessing

I hope you come to find
that which gives life a deep meaning for you.
Something worth living for—maybe even worth dying
    for—
Something that energizes you, enthuses you,
And enables you to keep moving ahead.

I can't tell you what it might be—
That's for you to find, to choose, to love.
I can just encourage you to start looking,
And support you in the search.

Sister Ita Ford, M.M.
(murdered in El Salvador in 1980)

May I be a healing grace in the lives of others,
May my joy and peace be a leaven to all I meet,
May I readily admit when the path becomes crooked in
    my own life,
May I join hands with my brothers and sisters in good
    times and bad,
May I be the Christlike witness to which you have called
    me,
This I ask in your name. Amen.

Aurelia C. Kulik, Purcellville, Virginia,
a friend of Maryknoll

A Prayer for Those Who Serve

Father of all, Lord of creation, please guide and bless the missioners, priests, sisters, brothers, doctors, nurses, and teachers—all who dedicate their lives to your service. Bless their work throughout this world. Pour out your Holy Spirit upon them, strengthen them in weakness, comfort them in trials. Be at their side in all their labor and joys. Open the minds and hearts of all to the message in your Gospel preached and lived by your missioners and witnessed by the joy of their lives.

Grant them a soaring spirit of love and health in body and mind that they may by their life and work discover the true message of peace, love and justice among those with whom they live. May their lives give witness to the brotherhood and sisterhood that will make your name known and loved by all through Christ our Lord. Amen.

Lucille Koda, Stamford, Connecticut,
a friend of Maryknoll,
from an old Maryknoll prayer booklet

Lord, somewhere in the missions a young man feels the call to be your priest. With all his heart he wants to serve you and to bring people to the faith that sustains me even at this moment. Give him all he needs to be a good priest. Make him holy, give him wisdom, bless him with compassion and, through him, help others to find you. Help me also, to be your missionary, here today, right where I am. Amen.

Mary Weiden, Narrowsburg, New York,
a friend of Maryknoll

Pack nothing.
Bring only
your determination
to serve and
your willingness to be free.

Only surrender to the need
of the time—to love
justice and walk humbly
with your God.

Set out in the dark.
I will send fire
to warm and encourage you.
I will be with you in the fire
and I will be with you in the cloud.

You will learn to eat new food
and find refuge in new places.
I will give you dreams in the desert
to guide you safely home to that place
you have not yet seen.

The stories you tell
one another around the fires
in the dark will make you
strong and wise.

You will get to where you are going
by remembering who you are.
Touch each other and keep telling stories.

Sharon Raynor, MMAF (Venezuela),
Maryknoll, New York,
from "Passover Remembered"
by Alla Bozarth-Campbell

O God, we call you by your name and we ask that your Son Jesus will be with us now. We are united here to remember and to praise you for the gifts you have given us in the life testimony of Dorothy, Jean, Maura and Ita. They have revealed your presence in the midst of our world broken by injustice, poverty and violence. They have shown us your love and have left us a challenge: to look for the truth, to love the poor not as objects of charity but as subjects of their own history, and to commit our faith to the urgent work of justice.

Help us to appreciate this faith by living it fully, listening to the challenges without fear, prepared to follow the footsteps of our martyrs. We ask this in Jesus' name. Amen.

Sister Josephine Lucker, M.M.,
San Salvador, El Salvador,
from a prayer written by
Sister Teresa Alexander, M.M.,
that was prayed at Santiago Nonualco,
where the four churchwomen were martyred.

Almighty God, in whom we live and move and have our being, you have made us for yourself and our hearts are restless until in you they find their rest. Grant us purity of heart and strength of purpose, that no selfish passion may hinder us from knowing your will, no weakness from doing it; but that in your light we may see light clearly, and in your service we may find our perfect freedom; through Jesus Christ our Lord.

St. Augustine (354–430)

Five Great Gifts of God

I. O Lord, give me the *ears* that can hear the cries for mercy and a gentle hand to ease their pain.

II. O Lord, give me the *eyes* to see the hate and prejudice around me and the courage to do something about it.

III. O Lord, give me the sense of *smell* that I can smell the sweetness of your creation and block out the stench of evil so I can love all without prejudice.

IV. O Lord, give me a *tongue* that I can speak the words of comfort to those in need when no one else knows the words to speak.

V. O Lord, give me the sense of *touch* that I can lay my hands on those in pain, and they will know through my touch that you, my Jesus, are with them.

But most of all, Lord Jesus, give me the gift of love so I can honor, love, and serve you on this earth and be happy with you in heaven.

Elizabeth V. Poole, Stevensville, Maryland,
a friend of Maryknoll, written after the death
from AIDS of a young man
disowned by his family

All for Jesus, for Jesus alone. Amen.
(What could be simpler than this? It dedicates our efforts to Jesus in some small attempt to repay him for all he did for us.)

Joe Corcoran, Industry, Pennsylvania,
a friend of Maryknoll

Faith

Thank you, God, for blessing me with faith.
Increase it, so I can never doubt.
Increase it, for the sake of those without faith.
Make me an instrument of your faith, for those with only
    a little.
Fill my body with faith, that I may work for you all my
    days.
Let me never be miserly, so I cannot refuse you anything.
In your hands, I am secure.
Hasten into my heart and remain there forever. Amen.

A Maasai prayer, Tanzania

Love

Heavenly Father,
We love you with our whole being.
Our being is in your being.
Our spirit is rooted in your spirit.
Fill us with love.
Let us be bound with others in
Love, as we go our diverse ways.
Let us be united in this one
Spirit, which makes you present
In the world, and makes you
Witness to the ultimate reality,
Love. We pray that love overcomes.
That love is victorious. Amen.

A Maryknoller in Thailand,
adapted from a prayer of Thomas Merton

Generosity

God, grant me generosity
Of spirit. Let me not
Think solely of myself today, but
Make the effort and take the time
To touch another's life.

Let me reach out to perform at
Least one kind act, to smile, to
Listen, to embrace. Grant that I
May live this day spreading joy
Among my brothers and sisters
In Christ, in fulfillment of the
Gospel's command to love one
Another.

Jackie Ring, from a Maryknoll prayer booklet

Morning Light

Dear God,
As first light streams
Through my window, and birds
Are singing to the dawn.
I rejoice that you have granted
Me another day of life.

Let me use your gift to laugh,
To love, to show compassion,
To work, to pray, to give.

Grant that I will reflect your
Light in all I do and say this day.

A Maryknoll Lay Associate

Oh, with a gesture light and free,
Lord, I would give my life to thee.
Not solemnly, nor grudgingly,
But I would take and fling it at thy feet,
And sing and sing
So that I may bring thee this small thing.

Sister Sarah Fogarty, M.M., Monrovia, California,
from a prayer by Mary Dixon Thayer

Holy Beautiful Lord, penetrate the darkness of my heart
with your light.
Give me true faith, unyielding hope, love without limits,
internal not external humility, together with Your wisdom
and understanding that is true.
So that, O Lord, I may do the things that You command,
that I may do Your will, not mine. Amen.

Father Jim Travis, M.M., Maryknoll, New York,
a daily prayer of St. Francis of Assisi

"God has yet a great work for us to do, but the
realization of this vision depends on you and me
as individuals and on our cooperation. Do we love
enough, do we work enough, do we pray enough,
do we suffer enough? Maryknoll's future depends
on our answer."

❧ *Mother Mary Joseph Rogers,*
foundress of the Maryknoll Sisters

In a time of drastic change,
>One can be too preoccupied
>With what is ending
>Or too obsessed with what seems
>To be beginning

In either case, one loses touch
>With the present
>And with its obscene
>And dynamic possibilities

What really matters is openness,
>Readiness,
>Attention,
>Courage to face risk

You do not need to know
>Presently what is happening,
>Or exactly where it is all going

What you need
>Is to recognize the possibilities
>And challenges
>Offered by the present moment,
>And to embrace them with courage,
>Faith,
>And hope

In such an event,
>Courage is the authentic form
>Taken by love.

Author unknown

Into Your Hands

Into your hands I place my life, O God
Take me and plant me like a seed.

Deep in the earth does the acorn know what it will be?
The seed breaks open and dies
in order to become what is unknown
but intended all along.
So we each live in the darkness of our own night.
Seeds in our shells, we must die to ourselves,
in order to come to new light.

So, O God, plant me deep in your love,
break me open to see me free.

High on the hill, rain falls into a stream.
It flows to the river and then to the sea.
Like water on water, we are one
and we join with our own.
As we're loved by the Father,
we love one another.
This is the journey home.

Pilgrims at heart, we hear God's call.
The journey is all.
Love is the way to begin.

So into your hands, I place my life, O God.
Take me and plant me like a seed.

Vicki Armour-Hileman, MMAF,
Maryknoll, New York

Lord, make us builders of an order that is guided by the justice and cordiality that can bring peace to the world. Give us a sense of dynamic equilibrium so your peace may be in our intentions, in the means we use, and in the ends for which we yearn. Amen.

Leonardo Boff, Brazil,
from The Prayer of Saint Francis
(Orbis Books, 2001)

Feasting in the Spirit

Spirit of God, move me,
   motivate me,
inspire me to rejoice always
   in the gifts you bring

Spirit of Jesus,
   in my hands, feet, mouth,
      heart, speech, action,
   let my very being
   pulsate with your life.

Spirit of God
   all around us and acting through us,
   lead us to freedom
   as we soar to new heights.
Give us courage and strength,
   teach us to lose ourselves in your Self
and become eternally one in peace.

Father Michael D. Bassano, M.M.,
Bangkok, Thailand

Prayer to the Holy Spirit

Come, Holy Spirit, breathe down upon our troubled world.
Shake the tired foundations of our crumbling institutions.
Break the rules that keep you out of all our sacred spaces.
And from the dust and rubble, gather the seedlings of a
      new creation.

Come, Holy Spirit, enflame once more the dying embers
      of our weariness.
Shake us out of our complacency.
Whisper our names once more, and scatter your gifts of
      grace with wild abandon.
Break open the prisons of our inner being
And let your raging justice be our sign of liberty.

Come, Holy Spirit, and lead us to places we would rather
      not go.
Expand the horizons of our limited imaginations.
Awaken in our souls dangerous dreams for a new tomor-
      row,
And rekindle in our hearts the fire of prophetic enthusi-
      asm.

Come, Holy Spirit, whose justice outwits international
      conspiracy,
Whose light outshines spiritual bigotry,
Whose peace can overcome the destructive potential of
      warfare,
Whose promise invigorates our every effort
To create a new Heaven and a new Earth,
Now and forever. Amen.

Father Leo Shea, M.M., Maryknoll, New York,
from a poem by Diarmuid O'Murchu

There is no pain too agonizing, no suffering too severe,
No sorrow too heartbreaking, no humiliation too shame-
    ful,
No poverty too depriving, no work too exhausting,
That I will not bless it, thank God for it, submit to it,
Embrace it and be crucified to it—
For the cause of Christ, for the honor and glory to God,
For the love and salvation of His people.
For nothing, no, nothing is greater than the love of God.

Elizabeth (Betty) Keller,
MMAF alumna,
Oaxaca, Mexico

Govern all by your wisdom, O Lord, so that my soul may
always be serving you according to your will, and not as I
desire. Do not punish me, I pray, by granting what I want
and ask, if it offends your love, which would always live in
me. Let me die to myself, that I may serve you, let me live
to you, who in yourself are the true Life.

St. Teresa of Avila (1515–1582)

O God, I give you everything of today:
every thought, word, deed,
emotion, heartbeat, blink of
my eyes, footstep and breath
for your honor, glory and praise. Amen.

Mary Jane Dougherty, Johnstown, Pennsylvania,
a friend of Maryknoll

I sought my soul,
but my soul I could not see.
I sought my God,
but my God eluded me.
I sought my brother,
and I found all three.

Mary Burke, Staten Island, New York,
a friend of Maryknoll, author unknown

Help me, O Lord, that my eyes may be merciful, so that I may never suspect or judge from appearances but look for what is beautiful in my neighbors' souls and come to the rescue.

Help me, O Lord, that my hands may be merciful and filled with good deeds, so that I may do only good to my neighbor and take upon myself the more difficult and toilsome tasks.

Help me that my feet be merciful, so that I may hurry to assist my neighbor, overcoming my own fatigue and weariness. My true rest is in the service of my neighbor.

Help me, O Lord, that my heart may be merciful, so that I myself may feel all the sufferings of my neighbor. I will refuse my heart to no one. I will be sincere even with those who will abuse my kindness, and I will lock myself up in the most merciful heart of Jesus. I will bear my own sufferings in silence. May your mercy, O Lord, rest upon me.

O my Jesus, transform me into yourself, for you can do all things. Amen.

Joan DeMellier, Waldoboro, Maine,
a friend of Maryknoll, from a prayer card
of the Association of Marian Helpers

A Prayer for Renewal

Father, we are your people, the sheep of your flock.
Heal the sheep who are wounded,
Touch the sheep who are in pain,
Clean the sheep who are soiled,
Warm the lambs who are cold.

Father, help us to know you through Jesus, the shepherd,
And through your Holy Spirit.
Help us to lift up that love and show it all over the world.
Help us to build love on justice and justice on love.
Help us to believe mightily, hope joyfully, love divinely.
Renew us that we may help renew the face of the earth.

Regina Motreuil, Ozone Park, New York,
a friend of Maryknoll, a prayer said daily for
Maryknoll missioners and the people they serve

Lord Jesus Christ, Son of the Living God,
show us your face.
We long to know you, in spirit and in truth,
for you are the Way to freedom.
Teach us to love your people,
as you and the Father love them,
to be slow to anger and rich in mercy.
Help us to understand ourselves,
to cherish your life within us
that we may become as you were,
a place of refuge for the lonely, the wounded and the sinner.

Sheila Cassidy, England,
from Good Friday People
(Orbis Books, 1995)

A Prayer for Service

May I, through whatever good I have accomplished,
Become one who works for the complete alleviation
of the suffering of all beings.

May I be medicine for the sick;
May I be their physician and attend to them
Until their disease no longer recurs.

May I be an inexhaustible storehouse for the poor;
And may I always be the first in being ready to serve them
    in various ways.

May I be a protector for the unprotected,
A guide for the travelers on their way,
A boat, a bridge, a means of crossing for those who seek
    the other shore.

For all creatures, may I be a light for those who need a light,
A bed for those who need a bed,
And a servant for those who need a servant.

> *Peggy Santos, San Diego, California,*
> *a Maryknoll Affiliate, a Buddhist prayer*
> *of the Bodhicharyavatara of Shantideva*

Dear Lord Jesus, please save us from apparent charity
that is disguised injustice, whereby we give to others out
of our "benevolence" what is their due in justice. Deliver
us from almsgiving that becomes a subterfuge. Amen.

> *Peter Murray, Brookfield, Wisconsin,*
> *a friend of Maryknoll,*
> *paraphrased from Father Pedro Arrupe, S.J.*

Dear Jesus, help me to spread your fragrance everywhere I go. Flood my soul with your spirit and life. Penetrate and possess my whole being so utterly that all my life may be only a radiance of yours. Shine through me, and be so in me that every soul I come in contact with may feel your presence in my soul.

Let them look up and see no longer me—but only Jesus. Stay with me. Then I shall begin to shine as you do: so to shine as to be a light to others. The light, O Jesus, will be all from you, none of it will be mine; it will be you shining on others through me.

Let me thus praise you in the way you love best, by shining on those around me.

Let me preach you without preaching, not by words but by my example, by the catching force, the sympathetic influence of what I do, the evident fullness of the love my heart bears to you. Amen.

Helen Chylewski,
Tehachapi, California,
a friend of Maryknoll,
a prayer of Mother Teresa

Come, Lord,
work on us,
set us on fire
and clasp us close,
be fragrant to us,
draw us to your love,
let us run to you.

St. Augustine (354–430)

Make My Heart Like Yours

O Jesus, I understand that Your mercy is beyond all imagining, and therefore I ask you to make my heart so big that there will be room in it for the needs of all the souls living on the face of the earth.

O Jesus, make my heart sensitive to all the sufferings of my neighbor, whether of body or soul.

O my Jesus, I know that you act toward us as we act toward our neighbor.

My Jesus, make my heart like unto Your merciful Heart.

Jesus, help me to go through life doing good to everyone. Amen.

Judy Johnson, Monument, Colorado,
a friend of Maryknoll,
from the Diary of Blessed Faustina Kowalska

"We have the task of teaching by word and example the truths that others would avoid, of restoring and building up the faith that has been lost or weakened, of promoting unity among God's people, of sowing peace where there is discord or courage where there is weakness or fear."

❧ *Mother Mary Joseph Rogers,*
foundress of the Maryknoll Sisters

O Lord Jesus Christ, who didst say: "My yoke is sweet," and yet dost call upon us to take up Thy cross and follow Thee, grant us so to realize the gravity of these sayings, no less than their attractiveness, that we may ever make your yoke light by our love for one another and may ever carry Thy cross by combining our forces. And since we are debtors to all, make us to all such an example of love and meekness and holy joy that we may truly be the fragrance of Thyself. Grant that we may come to such a love for Thy good and blessed cross by daily dying to ourselves that we may pass through death rejoicing and may win Thee as our reward.

O Mary, Mother most gentle, surround us with the warmth of thy love, throw over us the mantle of thy protection, and direct our steps to Him who is blessed above all forever. Amen.

Sister M. Elenita M. Barry, M.M.,
Stockton, California, from a prayer
of Fathers Anthony Cotta
and Vincent Lebbe (1898)

Come, Lord

Do not smile and say
you are already with us.
Millions do not know you
and to us who do,
what is the difference?
What is the point
of your presence
if our lives do not alter?
Change our lives, shatter
our complacency.

Make your word
flesh of our flesh,
blood of our blood
and our life's purpose.
Take away the quietness
of a clear conscience.
Press us uncomfortably.
For only thus
that other peace is made,
your peace.

Dom Helder Câmara, Recife, Brazil,
from The Desert Is Fertile
(Orbis Books, 1974)

Following Jesus
Does not mean slavishly copying His life.
It means making His choice of life your own
Starting from your own potential
And in the place where you find yourself.
It means living for the values
For which Jesus lived and died.

If there is anything in which this life,
This way, can be expressed, in which
God has been revealed most clearly,
It is the reality of love.
You are someone only in as far as you are love
And only what has turned to love in your life
Will be preserved.
What love is you can learn from Jesus.

So be converted to love every day.
Change all your energies, all your potential,
Into selfless gifts for the other person.
Then you yourself will be changed from
Within and through you God's Kingdom will
Break into the world.

∽ *From Maryknoll's Rule for a New Brother*

The Work to Build the Kingdom of God Continues

It helps now and then to step back and take the long view.

The Kingdom of God is not only beyond our efforts, it is
even beyond our vision.
We accomplish in our lifetime only a tiny fraction of the
magnificent enterprise that is God's work.
Nothing we do is complete, which is another way of saying that the kingdom always lies beyond us.

No statement says all that could be said.
No prayers fully express our faith.
No confession brings perfection.
No pastoral visit brings wholeness.
No program accomplishes the Church's mission.
No set of goals and objectives includes everything.
This is what we are about.
We plant the seeds that one day will grow.
We water seeds already planted, knowing that they hold
future promise.
We lay foundations that will need further development.
We provide yeast that produces effects far beyond our
capabilities.
We cannot do everything, and there is a sense of libera-
tion in realizing that.
This enables us to do something, and to do it very well.

It may be incomplete, but it is a beginning, as step along
the way,
An opportunity for the Lord's grace to enter and do the
rest.

We may never see the end results, but that is the difference between the master builder and the worker.
We are workers, not master builders, ministers, not
messiahs.
We are prophets of a future not our own. Amen.

Father Steve Judd, M.M., Puno, Peru,
a prayer of Archbishop Oscar Romero

*This commitment prayer was offered in 1987 by the Good
Shepherd Faith Community, Shawnee, Kansas, the Sisters of
Charity of Leavenworth, Kansas, and a community in Tres
Ceibas, El Salvador, called La Esperanza.*

Gentle and loving God, help
us to use our humanity and
faith as a golden thread uniting our hearts and hands as
we journey together. Send
us your Spirit to guide us on
this journey. Grant us the
strength to continue our
loving bond.

Gentil y bondadoso Señor,
ayudanos en usar nuestra
humanidad y fe, como un
hilo de oro que una nuestras
corazones y manos a viajar
juntos. Envianos tu Espíritu
para que nos guie en este
viaje y danos la fuerza de
continuar nuestra union de
amor.

Brother Mark Gruenke, M.M., Houston, Texas

A Prayer of Hope for the World

Lord God, we come to you in our need;
create in us an awareness of the massive
and seemingly irreversible proportions of the crisis we face
     today
and a sense of urgency to activate the forces of goodness.
Where there is blatant nationalism,
let there be a global, universal concern;
Where there is war and armed conflict,
let there be negotiation;
Where there is stockpiling,
let there be disarmament;
Where people struggle toward liberation,
let there be non-interference;
Where there is consumerism,
let there be a care to preserve the earth's resources;
Where there is abundance,
let there be a choice for a simple lifestyle and sharing;
Where there is reliance on external activism,
let there be a balance of prayerful dependence on you,
     O Lord;
Where there is selfish individualism,
let there be an openness to community;
Where there is the sin of injustice,
let there be guilt, confession, and atonement;
Where there is paralysis and numbness before the enor-
     mity of the problems,
let there be confidence in our collective effort.

Lord, let us not so much be concerned to be cared for as
     to care,
not so much to be materially secure as to know that we are
     loved by you.

Let us not look to be served,
but to place ourselves at the service of others whatever
  cost to self-interest,
for it is in loving vulnerability that we, like Jesus,
experience the fullness of what it means to be human.
And it is in serving that we discover the healing springs of
  life
that will bring about a new birth to our earth and hope to
  the world. Amen.

Marc LaClair, Oviedo, Florida,
a friend of Maryknoll,
from a prayer by an unknown author

Guidance

Guide me in your truth and teach me, for you are God my Savior, and my hope is in you all day long.
PSALM 25:5

The LORD will guide you always; he will satisfy your needs in a sun-scorched land and will strengthen your frame. You will be like a well-watered garden, like a spring whose waters never fail.
ISAIAH 58:11

How often do we seek the right path through life, yet go astray? Or perhaps we know which path is right but don't have the courage or the strength to follow it. Even though we have sight, we can't see the Way.

We seek wisdom, understanding, and assurance, along with peace and love. This is why we turn to God. Let us pray.

❧

God, I offer myself to you—to build with me and to do with me as you will. Relieve me of the bondage of self, that I may better do your will. Take away my difficulties, that victory over them may bear witness to those I would help of your power, your love, and your way of life. May I do your will always!

Jim Woolway, Chula Vista, California,
a friend of Maryknoll

Lord, Guide Me

If you try me,
send me out
into the foggy night,
so that I cannot see
my way.
Even if I stumble,
this I beg, that I
may look and smile
serenely,
bearing witness
that you are with me
and I walk in peace.

If you try me,
send me out
into an atmosphere
too thin for me to breathe
and I cannot feel the earth
beneath my feet,
let my behavior
show people that they cannot
part me forcibly

from you in whom we
breathe and move
and are.

If you let hate
hamper and trap me,
twist my heart,
disfigure me,
then give my eyes
his love and peace,
my face the expression
of your Son.

Dom Helder Câmara, Recife, Brazil,
from The Desert Is Fertile *(Orbis Books, 1974)*

O God, our Creator, our Ancestor,
come between us, fill us,
until we be like Thee.

Sister Josephine Lucker, M.M.,
San Salvador, El Salvador,
from a traditional African prayer
(Sister Jo formerly served in Africa)

Father in heaven,
hear my prayer.
Keep my family
safe in your care.
Guide them, dear Lord;
don't leave them alone.
Love them, please, God,
as we do at home.

Stella Zelinskas, Belleville, New Jersey,
a friend of Maryknoll

An Olde English Prayer

Give us, Lord, a bit o' sun,
a bit o' work and a bit of fun;
give us in all the struggle and sputter,
our daily bread and a bit o' butter;
give us health, our keep to make,
and a bit to spare for others' sake;
give us too a bit of song and a tale
and a book to help us along.
Give us, Lord, a chance to be our goodly best,
brave, wise, and free our goodly best
for ourselves and others
till all learn to live as sisters and brothers.

Anne Vogel,
Randolph, New Jersey,
a friend of Maryknoll

Father in heaven,
give me the grace to hold, above all, my love for my
        neighbor.
Help me to remember that love covers a multitude of sins.
Guide me to practice hospitality ungrudgingly.
Teach me how to pray for others and with others.
Let me always employ the gifts you have blessed me with
for the good of others so that I may be a worthy steward
        of your many graces.
May you be glorified through Jesus Christ your Son, for-
        ever. Amen.

Bertha Perron,
Vergennes, Vermont,
from a prayer by Stephanie W. Hughes

Prayer of Trust and Confidence

My Lord God,
I have no idea where I am going.
I do not see the road ahead of me.
I cannot know for certain where it will end.
Nor do I really know myself,
   And the fact that I think that I am following
   Your will does not mean that I am actually doing so.
But I believe that the desire to please you
Does in fact please you.
And I hope I have that desire in all that I am doing.
I hope that I will never do anything
Apart from that desire.
And I know that if I do this,
You will lead me by the right
Road though I may know
Nothing about it.
Therefore, will I trust you
Always though I may seem lost
And in the shadow of death, I will not fear, for you
Are forever with me, and you will never leave me
To face my perils alone.

Father Tom Marti, M.M., Maryknoll, New York,
from a prayer by Thomas Merton from
Thoughts in Solitude *(Farrar, Straus & Giroux, 1958)*

Prayer for Discernment

God, if this is your will, help me.
If not, stop me.

Father Joseph Veneroso, M.M.,
Maryknoll, New York

A Prayer for Church Leaders

O God of Love and Justice,
Our Creator and Liberator,
You created the universe
Full of so much beauty and harmony.
But in these days in which we live,
Justice and equality between your people
No longer exist.

In this year of jubilee,
We pray and struggle
To restore your dream
Of true justice and freedom for all.
We recognize that
We are co-creators and
Co-liberators with you.

And so we, your people, ask you
For the grace and strength
Of your Holy Spirit,
So that we may continue working
For a more just and peaceful world,
Full of love and happiness.

We ask all of this
In the name of Jesus Christ,
Our companion on the journey. Amen!

Father Dennis Moorman, M.M.,
João Pessoa, Brazil,
from a prayer by leaders
of the base Christian communities
in northeastern Brazil

Hymn of Universal Love

Let us cultivate a mind of boundless love
For all, throughout the universe,
In all its height, depth, and breadth,
Love that is unrestricted,
And beyond hatred or enmity.

Whether we stand, walk, sit, or lie down,
As long as we are awake,
Let us maintain this "love-awareness"
Deemed here a Divine State.

Holding no wrong view, virtuous,
And with vision of the Ultimate,
Having overcome all sensual desire,
Never in a womb are we born again.

*Father Jim Kofski, M.M., Bangkok, Thailand, from a
Buddhist prayer from Professor Kirti Bunchua, dean
of the School of Philosophy and Religious Studies at
Assumption University, Bangkok*

Almighty God,
Father of our Lord Jesus Christ,
establish and confirm us in your truth by your Holy Spirit.
Reveal to us what we do not know;
perfect in us what is lacking;
strengthen us in what we know;
and keep us faultless in your service;
through the same Jesus Christ our Lord.

St. Clement of Rome (c. 30–100)

A Prayer for Missions

O almighty God
Lord of all the peoples of the earth, we pray that you
guide and bless all those who go forth to preach the
Gospel in distant lands.
Pour out your Holy Spirit upon them.
Strengthen their weaknesses.
Embolden them with courage in their faith.
Comfort them in their trials.
Guide them in their actions to fulfill your divine will.
Give them the spirit of power and love to open the
hearts of those they serve to receive the good news.
We pray in Jesus' name. Amen.

Mary E. Maney, R.D.C,
White Plains, New York,
a friend of Maryknoll

Have no fear for what tomorrow may bring.
The same loving God who cares for you today will take
care of you tomorrow and every day.
God will either shield you from suffering or give you
unfailing strength to bear it.
Be at peace, then, and put aside all anxious thought and
imaginations.

Mary Ann Welsh, Ocean Pines, Maryland,
a friend of Maryknoll, from a prayer
of St. Francis de Sales (1567–1622)

Prayer for Generosity

Dearest Lord,
Teach us to be generous
Teach us to serve you as you deserve
To give and not to count the costs
To fight and not to heed the wounds
To toil and not to seek for rest
To labor and not to ask for any rewards except that of
       knowing
that we are doing your will. Amen.

Chip Cooke, Baltimore, Maryland,
a friend of Maryknoll,
from a prayer of St. Ignatius of Loyola

King's Son

Lord, isn't your creation wasteful?
Fruits never equal the seedlings' abundance.
Springs scatter water.
The sun gives out enormous light.
May your bounty teach me greatness of heart.
May your magnificence stop me being mean.
Seeing you a prodigal and open-handed giver,
let me give unstintingly, like a king's son,
like God's own.

Dom Helder Câmara, Recife, Brazil,
from The Desert Is Fertile
(Orbis Books, 1974)

Laying Down One's Life

Lord, you say there is no greater love than to lay down's
    one life for another.
Help us realize that there are many ways we can do this.

Help us to stand up and speak out instead of looking the
    other way when something is not just.
Help us not to judge others without knowing the road
    they have walked; instead, help us put ourselves in
    their shoes and try to understand their struggles.
Help us to use words that are affirming and encouraging
    instead of critical.
Help us to endeavor to be as honest as possible with the
    people we encounter and with ourselves.
Help us to seek to do good for all concerned instead of
    letting our egos get in the way of sharing.
Help us to build each other up instead of destroying with
    our words and actions.
Help us to bring a message of hope in the midst of struggles
    instead of despair.
Help us to be willing to let go and hold things loosely
    instead of grasping at possessions.
Help us to be willing to sacrifice for others instead of self-
    ishly grasping at what we want.
Help us love you, others, and ourselves, instead of only
    ourselves.

Give us the grace and strength to be able to live always in
    this way.

Iris Perez, Orbis Books,
Maryknoll, New York

Almighty God, who knows our necessities before we ask and our ignorance in asking: Set free your servants from all anxious thought about tomorrow; make us content with your good gifts; and confirm our faith that as we seek your kingdom, you will not allow us to lack any good thing; through Jesus Christ our Lord.

St. Augustine (354–430)

Purify, O Lord, my heart
Enlighten my understanding
Animate my will.

Claire J. Puttre, Baldwin, New York,
a friend of Maryknoll, from a prayer
learned in Catholic grade school
in Queens during the 1940s

Lord,
Help me to understand your plan.
We can't continue like this for very long.
Please intercede or make your presence known.
Please also show your mercy on our leaders.
Shed your grace, please, I pray, Lord. Amen.

Al Bruzzini, Sr., Maywood, Illinois,
a friend of Maryknoll

Grant unto us, O Lord, this day
    to walk with you as Father,
    to trust in you as Savior,
    to worship you as Lord;
    that all our works may praise you
    and our lives may give you glory.

Anonymous

A Prayer in Time of Distress

Lord, I'm in need of someone
to give me a hand and save me
and here you are with your hands
both nailed to a board.

I'm looking for somebody to walk with me
And I see your feet fastened to a cross.

I'm searching for a friend to claim
me as his own and I find you
with a bleeding heart.

I'm looking for life and I find
myself in the presence of a man who is dead.
Where shall I go for help, my God made man?

When Easter bells are ringing, they tell me
you died out of love and only
for three days . . . then you rose
to be my life and strength.

I beg you, my crucified and risen Savior,
Free me from selfishness and fear
to commit myself to justice.

Spare me from envy and worries.
Save me from resentment against
those who don't love or accept me.

Don't allow me to become callous
to the suffering of others
and to look only for my own comfort.

Free me from the boredom of my routine work
and from a life without meaning.

Lord Jesus, loosen my bonds through your cross
and give me strength and courage through
your resurrection. Amen.

Margaret H. Allocco,
Murrels Inlet, South Carolina,
a friend of Maryknoll,
from a prayer card of the Vocationist Fathers

Jesus, Lord of the sea and winds,
    calm the storm when we are frightened.
Jesus, Lord of the loaves and fishes,
    be our food when we are hungry.
Jesus, Lord of the lambs and flocks,
    seek us out when we are lost.
Jesus, Lord of signs and wonders,
    show Yourself when we have doubts.
Jesus, Lord of the blind and lame,
    take our hand when we grow weak.
Jesus, Lord of fields and flowers,
    care for us when others can't.
Jesus, Lord of all that lives,
    be our God; we are Your people.

William and Marilyn Bernhard,
Bancroft, Iowa,
friends of Maryknoll,
a prayer of Father Mark Link, S.J.

Litany of Humility

O Jesus! meek and humble of heart, hear me.

From the desire of being esteemed,
From the desire of being loved,
From the desire of being extolled,
From the desire of being honored,
From the desire of being praised,
From the desire of being preferred,
From the desire of being consulted,
From the desire of being approved,
Deliver me, Jesus.

From the fear of being humiliated,
From the fear of being despised,
From the fear of suffering rebukes,
From the fear of being calumniated,
From the fear of being forgotten,
From the fear of being ridiculed,
From the fear of being wronged,
From the fear of being suspected,
Deliver me, Jesus.

That others may be loved more than I,
That others may be esteemed more than I,
That in the opinion of the world others may increase, and
      I may decrease,
That others may be chosen and I set aside,
That others may be praised and I unnoticed,
That others may be preferred to me in everything,
That others may become holier than I,

Provided that I may become as holy as I should,
Jesus, grant me the grace to desire it. Amen.

Mrs. Robert H. Saehloff, Port Ewen, New York,
from The Pieta Prayer Booklet

Jesus, Help Me

In every need, let me come to you with humble trust,
saying Jesus, help me!
In all my doubts, perplexities, and temptations,
Jesus, help me!
In hours of loneliness, weariness, and trial,
Jesus, help me!
When others fail me, and your grace alone can assist me,
Jesus, help me!
When I throw myself on your tender love as a Father and
      Savior,
Jesus, help me!
When my heart is cast down by failure at seeing no good
      come from my efforts,
Jesus, help me!
When I feel impatient, and my cross irritates me,
Jesus, help me!
When I am ill, and my head and hands cannot work and I
      am lonely,
Jesus, help me!
Always, always, in spite of weakness, falls, and shortcom-
      ing of every kind,
Jesus, help me and never forsake me.

Ethel Galmarini, West Pittsburgh, Pennsylvania,
a friend of Maryknoll

Lord, help me to remember
that nothing is going to happen to me today
that You and I can't handle together.

John Kuper, Freehold, New Jersey,
a long-time sponsor and friend of Maryknoll,
anonymous

O God, tell me
what you want me to do
and give me the grace to do it!

Anne M. Mueller, Havre, Montana,
a friend of Maryknoll

Direct, O Lord, we beseech thee, all our actions and carry
them out by thy help, that every prayer, word, and work of
ours may always begin from thee and by thee be happily
ended.

Joan Holmden, Youngstown, New York,
a friend of Maryknoll, from a prayer
learned in high school in 1938

"When fearful about starting or doing something
difficult, I pray Peter's plea when he saw Jesus
approaching across the sea of Galilee: 'Lord, if it
is you, bid me come to you across the water!'
(Matthew 14:28)."

✍ *Marguerite Gomes, Newark, Delaware,*
a friend of Maryknoll

May I be an enemy of no one and the friend of what abides eternally.

May I never quarrel with those nearest to me, and be reconciled quickly if I should.

May I never plot evil against others, and if anyone plots evil against me, may I escape unharmed.

May I love, seek, and attain only what is good.

May I desire happiness for all and harbor envy of none.

May I never find joy in the misfortune of one who has wronged me.

May I gain no victory that harms me or my opponent. . . .

May I reconcile friends who are mad at each other.

May I, insofar as I can, give all necessary help to my friends and to all who are in need.

May I never fail a friend in trouble.

When visiting the grief-stricken, may I be able to soften their pain with comforting words.

May I respect myself. . . .

May I always maintain control of my emotions. . . .

May I habituate myself to be gentle, and never be angry with others because of circumstances.

May I never discuss the wicked or what they have done, but know good people and follow in their footsteps.

Warren Barshes, Palos Heights, Illinois,
a friend of Maryknoll,
a prayer of Eusebius of Caesarea
(A.D. 263–339)

God, I'm here. I'm not asking for anything, God. I just want to be near you and open my heart to you. I need you, Lord, and I am here at your disposal. Whatever you want to do with me, Lord, I am ready. I don't know what to say to you. I don't know what to ask you. I don't even understand what is important to me. You know all beforehand anyway. I know you have much to share with me, Lord, and I am finally ready to listen. Speak to me, Lord. My heart is open to you. But, Lord, please don't leave me alone.

Charles R. Graham, Miami Beach, Florida,
a friend of Maryknoll,
a prayer by Father Joseph Girzone
from Never Alone *(Doubleday, 1994)*

God of life,
there are days when the burdens we carry chafe our shoulders and wear us down;
when the road seems dreary and endless, the skies gray and threatening;
when our lives have no music in them,
and our hearts are lonely, and our souls have lost their courage.
Flood the path with light, we beseech thee;
turn our eyes to where the skies are full of promises. . . .

Flo Mangan, Springfield, Massachusetts,
a friend of Maryknoll,
a prayer by St. Augustine

Anima Christi

Soul of Christ, be my sanctification;
Body of Christ, be my salvation;
Blood of Christ, fill all my veins;
Water from Christ's side, wash out my stains;
Passion of Christ, my comfort be,
O good Jesus, listen to me.
In Thy wounds I fain would hide,
Ne'er to be parted from Thy side.
Guard me when the foe assails me;
Call me when my life shall fail me;
Bid me come to Thee above,
With Thy saints to sing Thy love, forever and ever. Amen.

Alphonsus Bell, St. Louis, Missouri,
a friend of Maryknoll,
translated by John Cardinal Newman

Lord, let me take each day as coming from you,
To give it back to you with your will complete.
And dear Lord, let me be kind.
Let me never be discouraged or feel sorry for myself,
Because you stand beside me every day.

Betty Fredericks, Warner, New Hampshire,
a friend of Maryknoll

"Don't pray when it rains if you don't pray when the sun shines."

❧ *Satchel Paige*

A Prayer to Jesus

Knowing you as my friend, I simply say, Jesus, I love you. When I am tired, I'll still try to say, Jesus, I love you. When I find it hard to forgive, I'll remember to say, Jesus, I love you. When darkness comes and I don't know where you are, I'll find you by saying, Jesus, I love you.

What trouble can shake me, what suffering can overcome me if I always repeat, Jesus, I love you? For the joys you give me, for the graces you grant me, my thanks will always be, Jesus, I love you. And when the evening of life comes and you invite me home, let me say one last time here below, Jesus, I love you.

Paula Wasser, Bourbonnais, Illinois,
a friend of Maryknoll,
a prayer in Maryknoll *magazine*

Lift mine eyes from the earth and let me not forget the uses of the stars. Forbid that I should judge others, lest I condemn myself. Let me not follow the clamor of the world, but walk quietly in my path. Give me a few friends who will love me for what I am, and keep ever burning before my vagrant steps the kindly light of hope. And, though age and infirmity overtake me, and I come not within sight of the castle of my dreams, teach me still to be thankful for life, and for time's olden memories that are good and sweet; and may the evening's twilight find me gentle still.

E. P. Hughes, Ishpeming, Michigan,
a friend of Maryknoll,
a prayer by Max Ehrmann given her
by a woman who lived to be 100

> "That is what prayer consists of, the recognition of our dependence upon God."
> ✺ *Bishop Francis X. Ford, M.M.*
> *from* Stone in the King's Highway
> *(McMullen Co., 1953)*

All highest, glorious God, cast your light into the darkness of my heart. Give me right faith, firm hope, perfect charity, and profound humility with wisdom and perception, O Lord, so that I may do what is truly your holy will. Amen.

Magdalene Reiger,
Ogden, Utah,
a friend of Maryknoll

Lord, it is hard sometimes to believe that you are really present in this world of ours. But I do believe it, Lord! Please help me live my life in such a way that it will be easier for others to recognize you.

When I find doubt, help me bring a little light. Where I find discouragement, let me be a ray of hope in the darkness. To those who feel estranged and alienated from you and your church, let me be as a bridge. When I meet those who have been hurt or misunderstood, help me leave only the imprint of your healing love and compassion.

Lord, wherever I go and to whomsoever I meet, help me be an instrument of your peace. Amen.

William E. Sermersheim,
Jasper, Indiana,
a friend of Maryknoll

Prayer for the Grace to Be Merciful to Others

Help me, O Lord, that my eyes may be merciful, so that I may never suspect or judge from appearances, but look for what is beautiful in my neighbors' souls and come to their rescue.

Help me that my ears may be merciful, so that I may give heed to my neighbors' needs and not be indifferent to their pains and moanings.

Help me, O Lord, that my tongue may be merciful, so that I should never speak negatively of my neighbor, but have a word of comfort and forgiveness for all.

Help me, O Lord, that my hands may be merciful and filled with good deeds, so that I may do only good to my neighbors and take upon myself the more difficult and toilsome tasks.

Help me that my feet may be merciful, so that I may hurry to assist my neighbor, overcoming my own fatigue and weariness.

Help me, O Lord, that my heart may be merciful so that I myself may feel all the sufferings of my neighbor and so that I will refuse my heart to no one. May Your mercy, O Lord, rest upon me.

Angela Demoret, La Porte, Indiana,
a friend of Maryknoll,
excerpted from The Divine Mercy Prayer Book

Let us not talk compassion when we continually practice
    intolerance.
Let us not espouse inclusiveness when we remain
    exclusive.
Let us not revel in our blessings when so many are
    without.
Let us remember that each of us in the world is God's
    child, with immense value in God's eyes.
Let us remember we are all pilgrims on the journey of life.
Let us remember we are all here for each other.
Let us remember we are all companions on the journey
    and accept one another.

M. Carol Ambuhl, Clifton Park, New York,
a friend of Maryknoll for more than thirty years,
following in the footsteps of her parents

For Serenity

Slow me down, Lord! Ease the pounding of my heart
by the quieting of my mind. Steady my hurried pace with
the vision of the eternal reach of time. Give me, amid the
confusion of my day, the calmness of the everlasting hills.
Inspire me to send my roots deep into the soil of life's
enduring values that I may grow toward the stars of my
greater destiny.

Helen T. Michalka, Fairfield, Connecticut,
a friend of Maryknoll,
a prayer by an unknown author

Dear God,
Empty my life of any stuff
   that brings clutter to my day;
Fill me with your powerful grace
   to lighten my pilgrim way.

Empty me of selfishness
   that appeals to false delight;
Fill me with a grateful heart
   that praises you day and night.

Empty me of those memories
   that deprive me of true peace;
Fill me with forgiveness and love
   so healing will never cease.

Empty me of anything that
   could obscure in me what's true;
Fill me with your Spirit-filled joy
   to live totally for you.

Sister Marie Roccapriore, M.P.F.,
Southington, Connecticut,
a friend of Maryknoll

O Lord, take Thou from me
All that makes me turn from Thee.

O Lord, give Thou to me
All that draws me nearer Thee.

O Lord, take myself from me.
Give me all and whole to Thee.

Marilyn Nowlin, San Antonio, Texas,
a friend of Maryknoll,
from Brother Klaus, Man of Two Worlds
by Christina Yates

Lord Jesus, may you yourself prepare
in the wilderness of our hearts the path of your return.
The hills of our pride—tear them down with your
humility.
The valleys of our despair—fill them with your hope.
The winding roads of our lives—straighten them with your
truth.
And let bloom in our desert the daffodils of your joy. Amen.

Josephine S. Fowler,
Downers Grove, Illinois,
a friend of Maryknoll

Prayer to the Holy Spirit

Come, Holy Spirit, replace the tension within me with a
holy relaxation;
replace the turbulence within me with a sacred calm;
replace the anxiety within me with a quiet confidence;
replace the fear within me with a strong faith;
replace the bitterness within me with the sweetness of grace;
replace the darkness within me with a loving warmth;
replace the night within me with your day;
replace the winter within me with your spring.
Straighten my crookedness,
   fill my emptiness,
   dull the edge of my pride,
   light the fires of my love,
   quench the flames of jealousy within me.
Let me see myself as you see me that I may see you as you
are.

Sister Suzanne Helmin, O.S.B.,
St. Joseph, Minnesota,
a friend of Maryknoll

Do not let the human in me spoil anything you give me to do. Push me back when I would go wrong and make me go forward when I am afraid to do right. Be with me in my dealings with each soul with whom I come in contact and grant that each may know, love, and serve you better for having passed me by.

Hilde Wendling, Port Charlotte, Florida,
a friend of Maryknoll, from "A Morning Prayer"

A Bengali Prayer

That You protect me in danger—this is not my prayer; let me not know fear when in danger.

I do not ask You to comfort me in the heart of sadness, in an aching state of mind; make me victorious over sadness.

Let not my strength break down when I find myself without a refuge. If I suffer any worldly loss, if I am repeatedly frustrated, let me not consider this harm irreparable.

That You come to save me—this is not my prayer; I ask for strength to overcome.

You need not comfort me by lightening my load; I ask for strength to carry my burden.

On days of joy, with humble head, I will remember You, I will recognize You.

On a dark, sad night, full of frustrations, oh, then may I not doubt You!

Cindy Pauldine, Oswego, New York,
a favorite prayer from Maryknoll *(July 1985),*
Gitanjali, "No. 4," by Rabindranath Tagore
(translated by Brother James Tallarovic, C.S.C.,
Dhaka, Bangladesh)

A Parish Prayer for Women

O God of Compassion, we pray for women everywhere. Make your presence known to those most in need of your comfort—the poor, the abused, and those who have no hope. Teach us who have so much to open our hearts and to be more aware of women who suffer, and let us never be afraid to speak out for the rights of the poor and the needy.

O God of Light, illuminate the dark places in our lives through the love of your son, Jesus. May his light shine with healing on abused women and children, on frightened pregnant teenagers, on desperate women in homeless shelters and on all who cry out for mercy and help.

O God of Wisdom, help us to look into our hearts where your Holy Spirit dwells and find the courage to minister to those who need us most. Give us guidance, strength, and dignity as we struggle in a flawed world to be good daughters, wives, mothers, grandmothers, and bearers of compassion in the name of our Risen Savior.

May we always remember that we can turn to you in prayer during times of crisis, and that you will answer us in the silence of our hearts and give us the knowledge and grace to live fully in the light of your truth. We offer our prayers and our hearts to you in the name of Jesus Christ, your Son. Amen.

Sara Muenster, Woodbridge, Virginia,
a friend of Maryknoll,
a prayer she wrote for her parish

Oh, only for so short a while
have you loaned us to each other,
because we take form in your act of drawing us,
and we breathe in your singing us.
But only for a short while
have you loaned us to each other,
because even a drawing cut in
crystalline obsidian jades,
and the green feathers, the crown feathers,
of the Quetzal bird lose their color,
and even the sounds of the waterfall
die out in the dry season.
So, we too, because only for a short while
have you loaned us to each other.

O Divine parent and Gift-giver,
let me not take those I love for granted,
failing to remember
that you have only loaned them to me
for a very short while.

Help me, this day, you who are absolutely love,
to love those you have loaned to me,
as if tomorrow you would call them home to you.
Let me not take them for granted
or be blind to the marvel of their presence,
to the sound of their voices,
the joy of their companionship
or the beauty of their love.

May their minor faults and failings
which often cause me discomfort
be seen as trivial transgressions
compared to the marvel of the gift
that you have loaned to me
for only a short while.

Margaret Wohlrab, Rochelle Park, New Jersey,
a friend of Maryknoll, from an Aztec prayer
to God (Edward Hays, Prayers for a Planetary
Pilgrim, *Forest of Peace Publishing, 1989.*
Reprinted with permission.)

Dear God,
Be good to me.
The sea is so wide,
and my boat
is so small.

Father John Halbert, M.M.,
Maryknoll, New York,
the Breton Fisherman's Prayer

Holy Spirit, come into my heart and soar to Jesus.

Marilyn Nowlin, San Antonio, Texas,
a friend of Maryknoll

Prayer to Be a Better Listener

We do not really listen to each other, God, at least not all
the time.
Instead of true dialogue, we carry on two parallel mono-
logues.
I talk. My companion talks.
But what we are really concentrating on is how to sound
good,
how to make our points strongly,
how to outshine the person with whom we are talking.
Teach us to listen as your Son listened to everyone who
spoke with him.
Remind us that, somehow, you are trying to reach us
through our partner in conversation.
Your truth, your love, your goodness are seeking us out
in the truth, love, and goodness being communicated.
When our words are harsh, hostile, angry, we convey the
very opposite of those qualities.
Teach us to be still, Lord, that we may truly hear our brothers and sisters . . .
and, in them, You. Amen.

Marianne Larson, Hickory, North Carolina,
a friend of Maryknoll

Dear Lord Jesus, fill my heart with your love
So you can do your work through me.

Camille Esperti,
Maryknoll Sisters Nursing Home,
Maryknoll, New York

Tolerance

Almighty God,
Help me remember that
You alone are perfect. You alone
Possess infinite patience.

When I expect perfection from
Myself, teach me humility.
When I seek perfection in others,
Give me patience.

Help me treat others as I would
Have them treat me, knowing
That we are all imperfect mortals.
Rid my mind of pride and power
This day and always. Amen.

Anonymous

Christ, open our hearts to the beauty of your love for us.

*Lena B. Caruso, Pittsburgh, Pennsylvania,
a friend of Maryknoll*

"Prayer does not change God, but it changes the one who prays."

Søren Kierkegaard

We Bless You, Father

We bless you, Father, for the thirst you put in us,
for the boldness you inspire,
for the fire alight in us,
that is you in us, you the just.

Never mind that our thirst is mostly unquenched
(pity the satisfied).
Never mind our bold plots are mostly unclinched,
wanted not realized.

Who better than you knows that success
comes not from us.
You ask us to do our utmost only,
but willingly.

Dom Helder Câmara, Recife, Brazil,
from The Desert Is Fertile
(Orbis Books, 1974)

Lord of the springtime, Father of flower, field and fruit,
smile on us in these earnest days when the work is heavy
and the toil wearisome; lift up our hearts, O God, to the
things worthwhile—sunshine and night, the dripping rain,
the song of birds, books and music, and the voices of our
friends. Lift up our hearts to these this night and grant us
thy peace. Amen.

Jay Allain, Hyannis, Massachusetts,
a friend of Maryknoll,
a prayer of W. E. B. Du Bois

Mary, teach me to use every moment of this new year for
       the love of God,
so that I may please him in all I do.
I do not know what this year will bring to my life;
what joys, what sorrows, what blessings, what crosses.
But in all that come to me,
let your hand, the hand that helped the infant Jesus,
always be held out to me.
Your hand will always comfort and soothe;
it will always protect me against harm,
for your hand but hides the hand of the all-powerful Christ.
His hand is in yours.

Where you are, blessed Mother, there is he.
I shall not more surely remain with him than if I cling to
       your hand.
Through you he comes to me.
Through you I come to him.

I ask for this grace: make me your child.
Looking up to you,
I shall ever see the light of Christ in your eyes;
following you I shall ever walk toward him;
faithful to you I shall always be faithful to him.

Jeanne Neilson,
a friend of Maryknoll

A Prayer of Mourning (September 11, 2001)

Almighty and ever loving God, in You we place our trust and hope. Violence and cruelty can have no part with You. You guide everything with wisdom and love. Hear the prayers we offer for those who lost their lives in the attack on America.

May Your love and the peace of our Lord Jesus Christ bless and console us and gently wipe the tears from our eyes and remove the fear from our hearts.

Look also with favor on the families and friends who mourn the victims and comfort them in their loss. Console them in the hope that all who trust in You will find peace and rest in Your Eternal Kingdom. Bless them with Your presence and surround us all with Your love.

Guide those in authority, O Lord. By the wisdom of our leaders and integrity of our citizens may harmony be restored and justice be served. Allow our leaders to strive in this time of despair for what is right and just.

Calm this terror that threatens us. Grant that peace, the fruit of justice and charity, may reign in America and throughout the World. Amen.

A prayer card of the Maryknoll Fathers and Brothers

The Power of Prayer

Nobody knows the power of prayer,
But somebody must be listening there
With a friendly ear for the heart that calls,
Someone who knows when a sparrow falls.

Miracles lie in the power of prayer;
Faith that can banish the soul's despair!
Hope that can shine like a holy light
And brighten the spirit's darkest night!

When earthly help is of no avail,
There is one Friend who will never fail;
Just lift your eyes—the answer is there,
For nobody knows the power of prayer!

❧ *Elizabeth Stlaurent,*
Chicopee, Massachusetts,
a friend of Maryknoll

Petitions

"Ask and it will be given you; search, and you will find; knock, and the door will be opened for you. For everyone who asks, receives, and everyone who searches finds, and for everyone who knocks, the door will be opened."
MATTHEW 7:7–8

Do not worry about anything, but in everything by prayer and supplication with thanksgiving let your requests be made known to God. And the peace of God, which surpasses all understanding, will guard your hearts and your minds in Christ Jesus.
PHILIPPIANS 4:6–7

Life can be hard. Sometimes guidance isn't enough. Instead, we need a miracle. The miracle of peace. A changed heart. A healed relationship. A new way of looking at something, or someone. Forgiveness. Reconciliation. For ourselves or for others.

Dare we ask? Yes, for scripture reminds us constantly to pray and reassures us that God indeed hears our prayers. Let us pray.

O Jesus, who has said, "Ask and you shall receive, seek and you shall find, knock and it shall be opened to you," through the intercession of Mary, thy most holy Mother, I knock, I seek, I ask that my prayer be granted. *(Make your request.)*

O Jesus, who has said, "All that you ask of the Father in my name, He will grant you," through the intercession of Mary, thy most holy Mother, I humbly and urgently ask thy Father in thy name that my prayer be granted. *(Make your request.)*

O Jesus, who has said, "Heaven and earth shall pass away but my word shall not pass," through the intercession of Mary, thy most holy Mother, I feel confident that my prayer will be granted. *(Make your request.)*

Gloria S. Richard, East Thetford, Vermont,
a friend of Maryknoll

Strength of Spirit

O Lord, may you always hear our prayers to break down walls. And may it always be you, Lord, who gives us the strength of spirit to come to our church, wherever it is and as it is. You know that whenever we are in prayer with you, Lord, we feel that strength of spirit and our hearts are filled with joy. Also, Lord, may we be prepared for the moment you knock on our door, that we may receive you with a happy smile. Amen.

Sister Joan Uhlen, M.M.,
Chacraseca, Nicaragua,
a prayer of Bertha Blauco
(translated by Sister Bernice Kita, M.M.)

No one, O my God, knows as you do how many things I need for soul and body, and you, all powerful and all kind God, have promised to give me what I ask for. Give me then a greater love for you and a stronger faith and a firmer hope. Give me the good judgment and strength I need to live as I should each day.

Give me the greatness of heart that will keep me from meanness and spite and ingratitude. Give me health and of this world's goods—enough, not too little or too much, and to my family and friends and to all people, grant peace, O Lord, and the will to worship you and to the souls of all, your everlasting light. Amen.

J. O'Dea, West Palm Beach, Florida,
a friend of Maryknoll

Health

Sun, O ancient Sun,
Immortal Father, Your work is
One of bringing health. Give us
Corn that nourishes, water that
Is life, wool to protect us from
The cold. Give us peace and
Justice and respect for this
Suffering people that is yours
And mine. Sun, my Father Sun,
Warm the air with your all-
Embracing flame. Let your
Strength come into our hearts,
And your might sustain our
Weakness.

A prayer from Peru

Give me a mind that is not bored
That does not whimper, whine, or sigh.
Don't let me worry overmuch about
That fussy thing called I.

Give me a sense of humor, Lord.
Give me the grace to see a joke,
To find some happiness in life,
And pass it on to other folk.

Betty L. Brehio,
Winchendon, Massachusetts,
a friend of Maryknoll

Grant, Lord God, that we may cleave to thee without
        parting,
worship thee without wearying,
serve thee without failing,
faithfully seek thee,
happily find thee,
and forever possess thee,
the one only God,
blessed for all eternity.

St. Anselm (1033–1109)

May my resentment be turned to gratitude,
May my straw be turned to gold.
May my vice be turned to virtue
So the glory of God may be told.

Elizabeth (Betty) Keller, MMAF alumna,
Oaxaca, Mexico

Father, give us wisdom to perceive you,
intellect to understand you,
diligence to seek you,
patience to wait for you,
eyes to behold you,
a heart to meditate on you
and a life to proclaim you,
through the power of the spirit
of our Lord Jesus Christ.

St. Benedict (480–547)

Give us, O Lord, a steadfast heart, which no unworthy
affection may drag downwards; an unconquered heart,
which no tribulation can wear out; give us an upright heart,
which no unworthy purpose may tempt aside. Bestow on
us also, O Lord, understanding to know you, diligence to
seek you, wisdom to find you, and a faithfulness that may
finally embrace you; through Jesus Christ our Lord.

St. Thomas Aquinas (1224–1274)

Lord of the Universe, maker of all:
tune our ears to hear your voice.
Speak to our hearts, we beg.
We dare you, Lord, to bid us "come,"
to walk to you across the water.
But if you do call,
give us courage,
for we are very scared
of getting out of the boat.

Sheila Cassidy, England,
from Good Friday People *(Orbis Books, 1995)*

Queen Liliuokalani's Prayer

When the Liturgy of the Mass is offered in Hawaiian, the Queen's Prayer, a penitential hymn, is part of the Penitential Rite and prayed before the Kyrie.

O kou aloha no,
Aia I ka lani,
A o kou oiaio,
He hemolele noi.

Oh, Lord, thy loving mercy,
Is high as the heavens,
It tells us of thy truth,
And 'tis filled with holiness.

Ko'u noho mihi ana,
A paahao ia,
O oe ku'u lama,
Kou nani ko'u koo.

Whilst humbly meditating,
Within these walls imprisoned,
Thou art my light, my haven,
Thou glory, my support.

Mai nana inoino,
Na hewa o kanaka,
Aka, e huikala,
A maemae no.

Oh, look not on their failings,
Nor on the sins of men,
Forgive with loving kindness,
That we might be made pure.

Nolaila, e ka Haku,
Malalo o Kou eheu,
Ko makou maluhia,
A mau loa aku no.
Amene.

For thy grace I beseech thee,
Bring us 'neath thy protection,
And peace will be our portion,
Now and for ever more.
Amen.

*Sister Kathleen Skenyon, M.M., Hawaii,
a prayer of Queen Liliuokalani composed
during her imprisonment in 1895 by the
missionary party that overthrew her
government, the Hawaiian Nation, in 1893*

Help your human creatures
to flee false riches
and plunge into the riches
for which all of us were born:
the one undivided love,
love of God and love of humankind.

Dom Helder Câmara, Recife, Brazil,
from Hoping Against All Hope
(Orbis Books, 1984)

O Lord, hear my plea. Have mercy on me. Help me in
my need for patience and kindness. I love you, O Lord,
and I place my needs in your hands. Thank you, Lord.

Mrs. Orland Oryall, Santa Maria, California,
a friend of Maryknoll

Come Holy Spirit. Here I am.
Touch me and make me whole.

William Burke, Beaverton, Oregon,
a friend of Maryknoll

"To those who love the Lord above, all things turn
out for good. And when God doesn't answer
prayer the way we wish God would, we must have
faith and patience when making our request, for
God will answer the way God knows is best."

✖ *Esther Irey, Waukomis, Oklahoma, a friend of*
Maryknoll (Esther, who is 93, apologized for not
typing but gives thanks that she can still write.)

Come Holy Spirit

Replace the tension within us
   With a holy relaxation.
Replace the turbulence within us
   With a sacred calm.
Replace the anxiety within us
   With a quiet confidence.
Replace the fear within us
   With a strong faith.
Replace the bitterness within us
   With the sweetness of grace.
Replace the darkness within us
   With a gentle light.
Replace the coldness within us
   With a loving warmth.
Replace the night within us
   With your day.
Replace the winter within us
   With your spring.
Straighten our crookedness,
   Fill our emptiness.
Dull the edge of our pride,
   Sharpen the edge of our humility.
Light the fires of your love.
   Quench the flames of our lust.
Let us see ourselves,
   As you see us,
That we may see you,
   As you have promised.
And be fortunate
   According to your word.
Blessed are the pure of heart,
   For they shall see God!

Author unknown

A Prayer in Time of Worry or Despair

This psalm recalls both the passion and resurrection of Jesus. It also reminds us that feeling abandoned is a common experience and that prayers are answered through our hope and trust in the will of God.

Eloi, eloi, lama sabactani!
My God, my God, why have you forsaken me,
   far from my prayer, from the words of my cry?
O my God, I cry out by day, and you answer not;
   by night and there is no relief for me.
Yet you are enthroned in the holy place,
   O glory of Israel!
In you our ancestors trusted;
   they trusted and you delivered them.
To you they cried, and they escaped;
   in you they trusted, and they were not disappointed.

Myrna Rodriguez, Social Communications,
Maryknoll, New York, from Psalm 22:20–26

Serenity Prayer

God, grant me the serenity to accept the things I cannot change, the courage to change the things I can, and the wisdom to know the difference. Living one day at a time, enjoying one moment at a time. Accepting hardships as the pathway to peace. Taking, as He did, this sinful world as it is, not as I would have it. Trusting that He will make all things right if I surrender to His will; that I may be reasonably happy in this life, and supremely happy with Him forever.

Ellie Hays, Maryknoll Affiliate, Sparks, Nevada,
from a prayer of Reinhold Niebuhr

Jesus, Help Me!

In every need let me come to you with humble trust, saying,
    Jesus, help me!
In all my doubts, perplexities, and temptations,
    Jesus help me!
In hours of loneliness, weariness, and trials,
    Jesus, help me!
In the failure of my plans and hopes; in disappointments,
       troubles, and sorrows,
    Jesus, help me!
When my heart is cast down by failure, at seeing no good
       come from my efforts,
    Jesus, help me!
When others fail me and your grace alone can assist me,
    Jesus, help me!
When I throw myself on your tender love as Father and
       Savior,
    Jesus, help me!
When I feel impatient, and my cross irritates me,
    Jesus, help me!
When sickness and loneliness overcome me,
    Jesus, help me!
Always, in weakness, falls, and shortcomings of every kind,
    Jesus, help me and never forsake me.

Florence Wratkowski, Minneapolis, Minnesota,
a friend of Maryknoll,
a prayer of Father Paul F. Peter

Take care of it, in your holy blessed name. Amen.

Jennifer Johnson, Eastchester, New York,
a friend of Maryknoll

Prayer to Christ the Healer

In the comfort of your love, this week, I pour out to you, my Savior, the memories that haunt me, the anxieties that perplex me, the fears that stifle me, the sickness and addictions that prevail upon me, the frustration of all the pain that is within me.

Lord, help me to see your peace in my turmoil, your compassion in my sorrow, your forgiveness in my weakness, and your love in my needs. Touch me, O Lord, with your healing power and grace. Amen.

Marlene McKinney, Charlotte, Michigan,
a friend of Maryknoll,
a prayer used at the
beginning of each meeting
of a parish support group

A Prayer for Healing

Divine Healer,
My body is tormented with pain
and my spirit is fearful.

I know that suffering is part of living
and that complete respite will come only when I rest with
 Thee.

Still, Merciful Father, take pity on me now
and restore me to health,
that I might regain my strength
and be able to accomplish good works,
in your name. Amen.

An anonymous Maryknoll Affiliate

Lord Jesus Christ, I'm upset and disturbed, and I pray that you will grant me the grace of inner peace; as you commanded the storm winds at sea to be calm, command the storms in my life to be calm. Give me the patience I need to cope with the burdens and the anxieties of my life. Grant me the strength to better deal with my problems, and the understanding to be more tolerant and kind to others; teach me to seek after your will, which alone brings peace of mind and peace of heart. Amen.

John and Margaret McCarthy, Seal Beach,
California, friends of Maryknoll

Note that for Africans, a God who saves tomorrow is not a saving God. God should save today.

(Name of deceased ancestor), look on your child and heal him/
her.
When? Today.
May your child give birth.
When? Today.
May the rain come.
When? Today.
May our cows give birth.
When? Today.
May we have well-being both in body and soul.
When? Today.
May all that is bad in our lives be thrown into the lake and
be eaten by the crocodiles. May we live in peace.
And may you, God, please help us.

Father Joseph Healey, M.M.,
Dar es Salaam, Tanzania,
from a Sukuma prayer for healing

Troubled Times

Savior Jesus,
I am beset with problems
And search for solutions. I feel
Overwhelmed by difficulty and
Cannot concentrate on the tasks
Which are at hand. My dispirited
Soul yearns for freedom from
Worry.

As you prayed in the Garden of
Gethsemane, "Father, remove this
Cup from me," so I pray that you
Will help me find a way through
These troubled times and that
Peace will be restored in my life.

A friend of Maryknoll

Prayer for My Spouse

Lord, bless and preserve my cherished spouse whom You have given to me. Let (his/her) life be long and blessed, comfortable and holy. Let me always be a blessing and a comfort to (him/her), a sharer in all (his/her) joys, a consolation in all the accidents and trials of life. Make me forever lovable in (his/her) eyes and forever dear to (him/her). Unite (his/her) heart to mine in fondest love and holiness, and mine to (him/her) in all sweetness and charity. Help us to laugh often. Help us grow in our love for each other and together in our love for You.

Helene Gillogly, Brevard, North Carolina,
a friend of Maryknoll,
a prayer given forty-eight years ago
to a 20-year-old bride

Prayer for Vocations

Lord Jesus, as you once called the first disciples to make them fishers of men, let your sweet invitation continue to resound: Come, follow me!

Give young men and women the grace of responding quickly to your voice. Support our bishops, priests, and consecrated people in their apostolic labor.

Grant perseverance to our seminarians and to all those who are carrying out the ideal of a life totally consecrated to your service.

Awaken in our community a missionary eagerness. Lord, send workers to your harvest and do not allow humanity to be lost for the lack of pastors, missionaries, and people dedicated to the cause of the Gospel.

Mary, Mother of the Church, the model of every vocation, help us to say "Yes" to the Lord who calls us to cooperate in the divine plan of salvation.

A prayer of Pope John Paul II

Prayer for Missioners

Remember our missionaries who give up all they have to testify to your gospel and love. Strengthen them in moments of difficulty. Crown their labors with the victories of the Holy Spirit. Through their endeavors, may your blessed name be made known throughout the world. Surrounded by an ever-growing number of your children, may they raise to you the hymn of thankfulness, redemption, and glory. Amen.

William E. Sermersheim, Jasper, Indiana
a friend of Maryknoll

A Prayer for Priests

O Jesus, I pray for your faithful and fervent priests; for your unfaithful and tepid priests; for your priests laboring at home or abroad in distant mission fields; for your tempted priests; for your lonely and desolate priests; for your young priests; for your dying priests.

But above all I recommend to you the priests dearest to me: the priest who baptized me; the priests who absolved me from my sins; the priests at whose Masses I assisted and who gave me your Body and Blood in Holy Communion; the priests who taught and instructed me; all the priests to whom I am indebted in any other way. O Jesus, keep them all close to your heart, and bless them abundantly in time and in eternity. Amen.

Mary Clare Callahan, Chesterfield, Missouri
a friend of Maryknoll,
from A Treasury of Prayers IV
(Leaflet Missal Company)

Dear God,
take the wheel with me that I may drive wisely and
     carefully,
that I may bring harm to no one or anything,
and that I may finish my journey safely. Amen.

Dorothea C. Metz, Dalton, Pennsylvania,
a friend of Maryknoll,
a prayer she says every time
she gets behind the wheel of her car

Prayer for Those We Love

I seek in prayerful words, dear friend,
my heart's true wish to send you.
That you may know that far or near
my prayerful thoughts attend you.

I cannot find a truer word
nor better to address you.
Nor song nor poem I have heard
is sweeter than "God bless you!"

God bless you! So I wish you all
of brightness life possesses.
For can any joy at all
be yours unless God blesses?

And so through all the days
may shadows touch thee never
But this alone, God bless thee,
then art thou safe forever.

Marie A. Zuniga, Spokane, Washington
a friend of Maryknoll, author unknown

A Sixty-Second Prayer for a Friend

Father, God bless *(name person)* in whatever it is that
you know *(he/she)* may be needing this day! And may *(name
person)*'s life be full of your peace, prosperity, and power as
(he/she) seeks to have a closer relationship with you. Amen.

Bill Medeot, Orbis Books,
Maryknoll, New York,
author unknown

What greeting shall I send you as I think of you today?
For the wish that I would wish you goes beyond what I
     can say;
Yet unspoken thoughts rise heavenwards in the silence when
     we pray.

I will breathe my intercessions before God's altar throne,
And the best wish I can wish you shall be told to him alone,
And the best thought I can send you is from him, and not
     my own.

And your name shall be remembered in the Blessed Pres-
     ence there
Where remembrances are sacred, and each memory holds
     a prayer
And where loving thoughts shall leave you in a loving
     Father's care.

Leone and John Cloepfil, Fort Benton, Montana,
friends of Maryknoll

The day was long, the burden I had borne
Seemed heavier than I could longer bear—
And then it lifted—but I did not know
someone had knelt in prayer,
Had taken me to God that very hour
And asked the easing of the load, and He
In infinite compassion, had stooped down
And taken it from me.

We cannot tell how often as we pray
For some bewildered one, hurt and distressed
The answer comes, but many times those hearts
Find sudden peace and rest.

Someone had prayed, and faith, a reaching hand,
Took hold of God, and brought Him down that day.

So many, many hearts have need of prayer:
Oh, let us pray.

Ellen M. Lyons, Peabody, Massachusetts,
a friend of Maryknoll,
from an old prayer card

Prayer of Spouses for Each Other

Lord Jesus, grant that I and my spouse may have a true and understanding love for each other. Grant that we may both be filled with faith and trust. Give us the grace to live with each other in peace and harmony. May we always bear with one another's weaknesses and grow from each other's strengths. Help us to forgive one another's failings and grant us patience, kindness, cheerfulness and the spirit of placing the well-being of one another ahead of self.

May the love that brought us together grow and mature with each passing year. Bring us both ever closer to You through our love for each other. Let our love grow to perfection. Amen.

Mrs. Raul Tuban, Gaithersburg, Maryland,
a friend of Maryknoll

"Prayer is not asking. Prayer is putting oneself in the hands of God, at his disposition, and listening to his voice in the depths of our hearts."

❧ *Mother Teresa*

Prayer of the Unemployed

Dear Lord Jesus Christ, you wanted all who are weary to come to you for support. Lord, I am worn out by my inability to find wage-earning work. Day after day, my worry and fear grow as the rejections of my applications mount. I am able and willing to work, but I cannot find a worthwhile job. Please help me to obtain one soon so that I can support myself and my family in a decent way. However, if it is your will that I wait longer, enable me to worry less and to be able to take advantage of the time available to get closer to you. Let me realize that there are other ways to bring about your kingdom on earth besides salaried work; help me to make use of them for the time being so that I may continue to grow as a person for your greater glory. Amen.

John and Margaret McCarthy,
Seal Beach, California,
friends of Maryknoll

May there be peace in your home because where there is peace there is love, where there is love, there is God, and where there is God, there is nothing lacking.

Aurelia C. Kulik, Purcellville, Virginia,
a friend of Maryknoll,
a prayer of a 10-year-old Guatemalan child

For Those Living Alone

I live alone, dear Lord,
Stay by my side.
In all my daily needs,
Be Thou my guide.
Grant me good health, for that I pray
To carry on my work from day to day.
Keep pure my thoughts, my every deed,
Let me be kind and unselfish in my neighbors' needs.
Spare me from fire, from floods, malicious tongues,
From thieves, from fear, and evil ones.
If sickness or an accident befall me,
Then humbly, Lord,
I pray, hear Thou my call.
And when I am feeling low or in despair,
Lift up my heart and help me in my prayer.
I live alone, dear Lord, yet have no fear.
Because I feel your presence ever near.

Nancy McDonald, Dunmore, Pennsylvania,
a friend of Maryknoll

Lord, I pray you to help me leave behind the past, to make
space to birth a new way of life. Amen.

Raul Mendoza, La Mirada, California,
a friend of Maryknoll

Prayer for the Sick

Dear Jesus, Divine Physician and Healer of the sick, we turn to You in this time of illness. O dearest Comforter of the troubled, alleviate our worry and sorrow with Your gentle love, and grant us the grace and strength to accept this burden.

Dear God, we place our worries in Your hands. We place our sick under Your care and humbly ask that You restore Your servant to health again.

Above all, grant us the grace to acknowledge Your holy will and know that whatsoever You do, You do for the love of us. Amen.

Bonnie Koenig, Belvidere, Illinois,
a friend of Maryknoll

Watch Thou, O Lord, with those who wake or watch or
      weep tonight,
and give Thine angels charge over those who sleep.
    Tend Thy sick ones, O Lord Christ.
    Rest Thy weary ones.
    Bless Thy dying ones.
    Soothe Thy suffering ones.
    Pity Thine afflicted ones.
Shield Thy joyous ones.
And all for Thy love's sake. Amen.

Bonnie Koenig, Belvidere, Illinois,
a friend of Maryknoll,
a prayer of St. Augustine

When Facing Surgery

My doctor has ordered me to surgery, O God.
It will be one of the rare times in my life
When I will relinquish all rights, all self-control,
The very beat of my heart into the hands of other human
      beings.
I am courting some apprehensions, my Lord.
I may manage to hide them from loved ones, but You know
      my fears,
as I prepare to gamble with uncertainty in the valley of
      shadows.
I don't have to be afraid. You have promised to stay by my
      side.
I lay claim to your forgiving and sustaining grace.
I commit my loved ones—and my own body and being—
      into your loving care.
Whether I awaken to carry on your purposes in this world
or enter into the eternal glory of your ultimate destiny for
      me,
This is in your hands, dear Lord;
I am content to leave it there, to pray that your will be
      done. Amen.

Flo Weiss, Breckenridge, Minnesota,
a friend of Maryknoll

A Prayer to St. Peregrine
for One Suffering from Cancer

Dear St. Peregrine,
I need your help.
I feel so uncertain of my life right now.
This serious illness makes me long for a sign of God's
love.
Help me to imitate your enduring faith
when you faced the ugliness of cancer and surgery.
Allow me to trust the Lord the way you did in this mo-
ment of distress.
I want to be cured, but right now I ask God
for the strength to bear the cross in my life.
I seek the power to proclaim God's presence in my life
despite the hardship, anguish, and fear I now experience.

I pray, glorious St. Peregrine,
be an inspiration to me and petitioner of these needed
graces from our living father. Amen.

Marina McClelland, Cleveland, Ohio,
a friend of Maryknoll,
author unknown

May the Divine assistance remain always with us, and
may the souls of *all* the departed, through the mercy of
God, rest in peace. Amen.

Dolores Davis, Cupertino, California,
a friend of Maryknoll (with a note that she was
told many years ago to pray for all *the departed,*
not just the "faithful departed")

Prayer for the Unity of Christians

O Lord Jesus Christ, who on the night of your passion prayed that your disciples would be one as you in the Father and the Father in you, may we feel with sorrow the evil of our divisions and truly discover and uproot every feeling of indifference, distrust and resentment within ourselves.

Grant us the grace to encounter all people in you, so that in our hearts and on our lips we may unceasingly raise your prayer for unity as you will, and by the means you will. Grant that we may find in you who are perfect love the way which leads to unity in obedience to your love and your truth. Amen.

Gloria Hutchinson
from O Odigos la Guida *19:1 (2000), 14.*
Reprinted in the London Tablet *in January 2002*

Petitions for Peace

O God, from whom all holy desires, all right counsels, and all just works proceed, grant unto thy servants that peace which the world cannot give, that our hearts may be set to obey thy commandments, and also that we, being delivered from the fear of our enemies, may pass our time, under thy protection, in rest and quietness. Amen.

The Maryknoll Missal, 1961

Prayer for the Harvest

God, possessor of all
Brightness,
You brought us rain,
And we have a good harvest.
Let us eat this grain calmly and
Peacefully. Save us against
Surprise or depression. Guard
Us against illness of people or
Our herds and flocks. Grant that
We enjoy this season's harvest in
Tranquility. Peace. Praise God.
Peace be with us.

Kenya

Invocation for National Prosperity

God, owner of all things,
I pray thee, give me what I need because I am suffering,
And also my children and all the things that are in this
            country of mine.
I beg thee for life, the good one with all I need;
Healthy people with no disease,
May they bear healthy children;
And also to women who suffer because they are barren,
Open fully the way by which they may see children.
Give goats, cattle, food, honey;
And also the troubles of the other lands that I do not know,
Remove them.

John Mbiti, Meru, Kenya,
The Prayers of African Religion
(Orbis Books, 1975)

A Prayer for Rain

God our Father, we come to you, kneeling at your feet, begging you to give us rain.

Your Son Jesus Christ tells us: Ask and you shall receive; seek and you shall find; knock and it shall be opened to you.

Now we are asking, we are seeking, we are knocking that you give us a big rain that we may get food in abundance, that there be water and grass for our cattle, that the year be one of peace, and that the danger of famine be averted.

Father, give it to us, help us. You know well that we must have rain. Give it to us! We promise you that we shall try to be good Christians, repent our sins, confess them and give them up, receive the sacraments and obey your commandments.

God, our Father, help us. Amen.

Father Richard A. Hochwalt, M.M.,
Shinyanga, Tanzania,
from a Sukuma prayer

To the Creator of nature and of humanity, of truth and
     beauty, I pray.

Hear my voice, for it is the voice of victims
Of all wars and violence among individuals and nations.

Hear my voice, for it is the voice of all children
Who suffer when people put their faith in weapons and
     war.

Hear my voice when I beg you to instill into the hearts
Of all human beings the wisdom of peace,
the strength of justice and the joy of fellowship.

Hear my voice, for I speak for the multitudes
In every country and in every period of history
Who do not want war and are ready to walk the road of
     peace.

Hear my voice, and grant insight and strength
So that we may always respond to hatred with love,
To injustice with total dedication to justice,
to need with sharing of self, to war with peace.

O God, hear my prayer
and grant unto the world your everlasting peace. Amen.

Shirley Cavagnaro, Tioga, Pennsylvania,
a friend of Maryknoll,
prayer of Pope John Paul II
at Hiroshima, 1981

Litany for Peace

In faith let us pray.

From every evil	*Deliver us, Lord.*
From acts of terror	*Deliver us, Lord.*
From all temptation	*Deliver us, Lord.*
From acts of violence	*Deliver us, Lord.*
From quarrel and strife	*Deliver us, Lord.*
From war and danger	*Deliver us, Lord.*
From thoughts of vengeance	*Deliver us, Lord.*
From all our sins	*Deliver us, Lord.*

For peace in our world	*Lord, hear our prayer.*
For peace in Afghanistan	*Lord, hear our prayer.*
For peace in Israel	*Lord, hear our prayer.*
For peace in Palestine	*Lord, hear our prayer.*
For peace in Africa	*Lord, hear our prayer.*
For peace in Asia	*Lord, hear our prayer.*
For peace in Europe	*Lord, hear our prayer.*
For peace in the Americas	*Lord, hear our prayer.*
For peace in our hearts	*Lord, hear our prayer.*

*A prayer card from the Maryknoll Fathers
and Brothers*

"Sanctify yourself, then you can sanctify society!"
❧ *Margaret Krest, Trenton, New Jersey,
a friend of Maryknoll, from St. Francis of Assisi*

Children's Prayers for Peace

Christmas is near and the people await the coming of Jesus, the Prince of Peace. But in 1986 the war in El Salvador continued, with no end in sight. These prayers show how some children expressed their desire for peace.

We Wish to Know Peace

I wish to ask you if you have seen peace pass by. They say that some time ago it passed by. I was very small and couldn't see it pass. I still wish to see it. *(Saul, Camp #7)*

How Wonderful It Is to Live in Peace

I would like to fly like the small birds that seek a nest in order to rest. In this prison, I am very sad, because my yearning is to live with my brothers and sisters, to be free like the wind, to sing with my friends, to live in my small house in El Salvador and to say to the entire world: How wonderful it is to live in peace. *(Eulalio, Josefa, and Elsa, Camp #6)*

Peace Boat

Small boat made of paper, my faithful friend, take me and sail me to all, with a voice of friendship: Peace. *(Santiago, Camp #2)*

*Father Paul Belliveau, M.M.,
San Pedro Sula, Honduras*

God, grant us wisdom.
Let us pray with one voice.

Praise You. Peace be with us.
Grant that our country may be
Tranquil, and our people may
Increase.

Praise You. Peace be with us.
Grant that our people, flocks and
Herds may prosper and be free
From illness.

Praise You. Peace be with us.
Grant that fields may bear much
Fruit and that the land may
Continue to be fertile.

Praise You. Peace be with us.

Kenya

In the quiet of the morning,
as I wake to start the day,
I feel God's peace around me and pray for it to stay.
I pray for peace within my home,
for peace among family and friends.
I pray for peace around the world,
from dawn until day's end.
In the silence of the sunrise,
I look toward heaven
and know that I must plant the seeds of peace
and tend them so they grow. Amen.

Catherine Zarembski,
Dearborn Heights, Michigan,
a friend of Maryknoll

Dear Lord,
We have felt the fear and the grief that hatred brings.
Help us to bond together as your people to heal the pain,
cherish the memories, and learn to celebrate our differences.
You created us all as your very dear children;
Teach us to live in the example of your only Son,
to live in faith, be confident in hope, act in charity,
and believe in the power of prayer.
Help us to find peace within our hearts and among
        all nations. Amen.

Bertha Perron, Vergennes, Vermont,
from a prayer by Alice Trumbull

"Despite the promise of Jesus to answer our sincere prayers, we've all met people (perhaps ourselves?) who complain that 'God may answer your prayer but God certainly doesn't answer mine.' When pressed, they may tell you how they repeatedly asked God for something very important to them, yet failed to ever get it. Therefore, God doesn't answer their prayer. In such cases what they ask for may be coming strictly from their own will with no reference at all to what God may want of them at this time in their lives. Such prayer merely consists in asking God to affirm their will and grant them what they've already decided on by themselves. That's not really God's role in our lives."

❧ *Father Donald McQuade, M.M.,*
from To Pray in That Secret Place
(St. Paul Publications, Philippines, 1989)

Lord, grant me peace and tranquility to pass along to the rest of the children who are like me. Make the grownups see that to come to you, one has to be a child, and that you are the only one who can bring justice and peace to the world. I ask you, for all those who want to be more than others and who are looking for their own gain, give them a heart for humanity.

For all of us, I ask that we can know how to get along as brothers and sisters, and know that we are all the same in your eyes—without size, color, race or religion mattering. Especially, I ask that we can respect others' rights so that we can all live as your children.

> *Barbara Hussey Riggins, Walnut Creek, California,*
> *a friend of Maryknoll, a prayer of*
> *Marcos Garcia Diego, a 10-year-old Mexican boy*
> *(used with permission of the Christian*
> *Foundation for Children & Aging, Kansas City)*

Dear Lord, hear my prayer today,
That peace in the world will come to stay.
Replace all killing and wars with love;
For this I pray dear God above.

Teach us to have patience and learn to forgive,
Those that we work with and with whom we live.
Fill up our hearts with love for others;
Start out first with sisters and brothers.
May peace in our families start today,
Then travel the world to remain there that way. Amen.

> *Anne Gauthier Kuetkosky, Edison, New Jersey,*
> *a friend of Maryknoll*

Lord, make us instruments of your peace as we seek to live in peace with ourselves, with the community closest to us, with others in our unequal society, and in the midst of the worst conflicts. May we be able to strive to bear tensions and contradictions, seeking to maintain communion with all creatures and making your peace visible. Amen.

Lord, where there is hatred let me sow love. Make us draw out of ourselves the love hidden under the ashes of secret hatreds. May our love for others stir up the love hidden within them that can transform hatred. Make love set our hearts on fire, shine forth in our attitudes, and be embodied in our actions, so that hatred will have no more place in us. Amen.

Where there is discord, let me sow union. Give us thirst for justice, understanding, and tolerance so that we may live joyfully with one another. Give us a heart that feels the beating of the hearts of the universe and of every creature, a beating that is in tune with your divine heart that unites all, diversifies all and makes all converge. Amen.

Lord, where there is error, let me sow truth. Grant that we may be courageous in uncovering our errors, especially those that obscure your presence in all things. May the truth shine through our sincere hearts, our humanizing gestures, our pure intentions, and our ongoing pursuit of fidelity and truth. Never allow us to oppress others in the name of religious truth. Amen.

Lord, where there is darkness, may I bring light. You are the true light that enlightens every person who comes into this world. Enable me through inspired words, consoling gestures, and a warm heart to dissipate human darkness so that your light may show us the way and bring joy to life. Amen.

O Master, grant that I may seek not so much to be consoled as to console. May I be able to emerge from my own pain to hear the cry of the one suffering beside me. May I have words to console and gestures to create serenity, confident surrender, and profound peace. Amen.

O Master, may I seek not so much to be understood as to understand. Grant that I may welcome others as they are. Only thus will I understand as I am understood. Grant that I may see the smallest sign of truth, goodness, and love in the other in order to strengthen it and enable it to come fully into the light. Amen.

O Master, often and in many ways you have forgiven us unreservedly, as a loving Mother forgives a child. Grant that we may also forgive those who have wronged us, and that we will never cease believing in generosity of heart, which can forgive even when unjustly wounded by many offenses. Amen.

Leonardo Boff, Brazil,
from The Prayer of Saint Francis
(Orbis Books, 2001)

Great and merciful God, Lord of peace and of life, your designs are for peace, not affliction. You sent your son, Jesus, to proclaim peace to those near and far and to reunite people of all races and descent in a single family. Hear the unanimous cry of your children, the sorrowful plea of all humanity for peace. Speak to the hearts of those in charge of the destiny of others. Stop the desire for retaliation and revenge; suggest with your Spirit new solutions, generous and honorable gestures, time for patient waiting. Grant to our times days of peace. Amen.

Catherine Gorecki, Foley, Minnesota,
a friend of Maryknoll,
based on a peace prayer
of John Paul II, January 16, 1991

Fiesta

It is a season of Joy
    occasion for song
    and dancing feet,
rhythms of our earth.

Ave Maria—
Paeans of Advent
    Mary the Dawn
    Christ the Mystic Vine
and memories of one's history.

Ave Jesu—
Greetings, gifts and garlands,
    moments of gladness
    sustain our senses
add strength to Spirit.

Faith, Hope and Love
    fill all creation
    with Presence of God,
give us the Gift of Peace.

Amen. Alleluia.

Sister Frances L. Venard, M.M.,
Maryknoll, New York

Lord, make me an instrument of your peace.
Where there is hatred, let me sow love.
Where there is resentment, let me bring forgiveness.
Where there is discord, let me bring harmony.
Where there is error, let me bring truth.
Where there is doubt, let me bring faith.
Where there is despair, let me bring hope.
Where there is darkness, let me bring light.
Where there is sadness, let me bring joy.
Master, let me not seek
to be consoled than to console,
to be understood than to understand,
to be loved than to love.
For it is in giving that we receive
it is in forgetting ourselves that we find ourselves
it is in forgiving that we are forgiven
and it is in dying that we rise to eternal life.

Written in 1913, this prayer has been attributed to
Saint Francis of Assisi

Our Daily Bread

*He was praying in a certain place, and after he had
finished, one of his disciples said to him, "Lord, teach us
to pray, as John taught his disciples." He said to them,
"When you pray, say: Father, hallowed be your name.
Your kingdom come. Give us each day our daily bread.
And forgive us our sins, for we ourselves forgive
everyone indebted to us. And do not bring us
to the time of trial."*

LUKE 11:1–4

Jesus asks us to "pray always." To pray always is to live in
the presence of God. Therein lies our safety, our peace.
This is life in "the secret place of the Most High" (Psalm
91:1). It is where we find our daily bread, all that sustains
our life.

Most of us live in a world of thoughts and restless anxiety. We need to still ourselves from time to time and be
mindful of the presence of God. Prayer can point the way
to where true life never ends. Let us pray.

❧

Lord, my God, the morning sky announces a new day.

Open not only my eyes, but awaken my heart to the mystery of Your presence in all the earth.

I arise to meet the challenges and surprises as yet hidden in the hours of this day. I arise also to embrace the mystery of the cross that awaits me in any troubles that may come my way.

May my efforts to walk in your footsteps be blessed as I place all the needs of this day in your hands. Amen.

Susie Giannoni,
Maryknoll Sisters, New York,
from prayers from Derry, Northern Ireland

God, thank you for giving me another day. Let me face my troubles today—the big and the small—with a happy heart filled with your unending love. Let me appreciate the moments of joy you send me this day. Let me see the cares of others as an opportunity to bring your great compassion to those who most need it. And, God, I know that you see and know all things—all of the world's loveliness, and all of its harshness too. So on this day that you have given me, I ask that I may bring your joy with me as I share myself with others. And I pray that you will be warmed by the happiness of your children. Finally, God, let me never forget that in all things, in gladness or sorrow, you who are all love and joy and hope are always by my side. Amen.

E. P. Hughes, Ishpeming, Michigan,
a friend of Maryknoll,
author unknown

Good Morning, God

You are ushering in another day
untouched and freshly new,
so here I come to ask You, God, if
You'll renew me too.

Forgive the many errors that
I made yesterday,
and let me try again, dear God,
to walk closer in Thy way.

But Father, I am well aware
I can't make it on my own.
So take my hand and hold it tight
for I can't walk alone.

Barbara G. Fetrow, Duncombe, Iowa,
a friend of Maryknoll,
a prayer by Helen Steiner Rice

For a Day Full of Blessings

O sun,
As you rise in the east through God's leadership,
Washing away all the evils of which I have thought
          throughout the night.
Bless me, so that my enemies will not kill me and my family;
Guide me through hard work.
O God, give me mercy upon our children who are suffering:
Bring riches today as the sun rises;
Bring all fortunes to me today.

John Mbiti, Kenya, a prayer of the Abaluyia
of Kenya from The Prayers of African Religion
(Orbis Books, 1975)

Morning Blessing

Lord, I thank you for the blessing of this new day. May I use it to reflect Your presence in all my thoughts, words, and actions, so that these hours might end with the world a little better place and someone's life a little happier because of my efforts. Amen.

Jean Robinson, Beaverton, Oregon,
a friend of Maryknoll

Dear Lord,
I need to thank you for keeping me healthy.
I want to offer you my daily words, actions and thoughts.
Please help me speak kind words, work and play whole-
    heartedly,
and have good thoughts about people.
I love to hear your promise through the rainbow:
"Don't be afraid, I am with you."

Joanna Eng, Montclair, New Jersey,
a friend of Maryknoll

"With my back against a bamboo post, legs crossed in lotus fashion and hands resting in my lap, I pass an hour with the Lord. Through the time I simply wait on God without book or beads in hand. Time passes peacefully; this 'wasting time on God' is the most reassuring exercise of the day."

◆ *Father Bob McCahill, M.M., Bangladesh,*
Dialogue of Life: A Christian among Allah's Poor
(Orbis Books, 1996)

Jesus Lord, I offer you this new day because
I believe in you, love you, hope all things in you
And thank you for your blessings.
I am sorry for having offended you
and forgive everyone who has offended me.
Lord, look on me and leave in me peace and courage
and your humble wisdom
that I may serve others with joy,
and be pleasing to you all day. Amen.

Ellen M. Lyons, Peabody, Massachusetts,
a friend of Maryknoll,
from a Franciscan morning prayer

Dear Jesus, make our hearts merry,
Our words joyful,
Our smiles broad and lingering.
May our actions be steeped in love,
And all our goals converge in you.
Fill our hearts with the brightness of hope
To shield us from the darkness of despair.
Listen to our songs of praise,
Forgive our weaknesses,
Bless us always and everywhere.

June Guncheon Vajda, Columbia, Pennsylvania,
a friend of Maryknoll

Another day you give me, Lord,
Another chance to know
Your gifts of peace and joy are mine
Wherever I may go.

Sister Marie Roccapriore, M.P.F.,
Southington, Connecticut,
a friend of Maryknoll

Heavenly Father, walk with me today,
and grant that I may hear your footsteps
and gladly follow where they lead.
Talk with me today
and grant that I may hear your tender voice and quicken
      to its counsel.
Stay with me today
and grant that I may feel your gentle presence in all I do,
      say, and think.
Be my strength when I weaken,
my courage when I fear.
Help me to know that it is your hand holding mine
through all the hours of this day.
And when night falls,
grant that I may know I rest in your sacred heart. Amen.

Cecelia Renschen, Aviston, Illinois, a friend of
Maryknoll (Cecelia is 92 and had been married for
fifty-one years when her husband died. Her
husband was one of twelve children and she was
one of fifteen. They never had children but have
ninety-two nieces and nephews!)

I come to you, Jesus, to take your touch before I begin my day. Let your eyes rest upon my eyes for a while. Let me take to my work the assurance of our friendship. Fill my mind to the last, through the desert of noise. Let your blessed sunshine fill my thoughts, and give me strength for those who need me.

Mary Elspeth Byers, Bella Vista, Arizona,
a friend of Maryknoll,
a prayer attributed to Mother Teresa

Lord, thank you for another day
   within this life of mine.
Give me the strength to live it well,
   whatever I may find.
Bestow from your abundance
   whatever I may lack.
To use the hours wisely,
   for I cannot have them back.
Lord, thank you for another day,
   in which to make amends
   for little slights or petty words,
   inflicted on my friends.
For sometimes losing patience
   with problems that I find.
For seeing faults in other lives,
   but not the ones in mine.
Lord, thank you for another chance,
   in which to try to be
   a little more deserving
   of the gifts you've given me.
For yesterday is over,
   and tomorrow's far away,
   and I remain committed
   to the good I do today!

Mrs. Henry Schleier, Jr., Mequon, Wisconsin,
a friend of Maryknoll

"'Give us this day our daily bread' is probably the most perfectly constructed and useful sentence ever set down in the English language."

∙ *P. J. Wingate*

The Best Day of My Life

This day when I awaken, I will remind myself that this is the best day of my life!

There were moments when I wondered if I would reach this day, but I have reached it and I am going to celebrate! Today I am going to celebrate what an incredible life I have lived until this moment: the achievements, the gains, the many blessings and, yes, even the difficulties because they have made me strong.

I will pass this day with my head held high and a happy heart. I will marvel at all the gifts of God: the simple things in appearance; the morning dew, the sun, the clouds, the trees, the flowers, the birds. Today none of these marvelous creations will pass without my taking note.

Today I will share my enthusiasm for life with other people. I will smile at someone. I will make it a habit to realize a gesture of kindness toward someone who does

El Mejor Día de Mi Vida

Hoy día, cuando me despierto, de pronto me doy cuenta de que este es el mejor día de toda mi vida.

Hubo momentos en los que me preguntaba si alcanzaría el día de hoy, pero ¡lo alcance! Y por haberlo alcanzado, voy a celebrar. Hoy, voy a celebrar que vida increíble he vivido hasta el momento; los logros, las muchas bendiciones y, sí, hasta las dificultades, porque ellas han servido para fortalecerme.

Pasaré este día con la cabeza en alto y el corazón feliz. Me maravillaré de los dones de Dios, sencillos en apariencia; el rocío de la mañana, el sol, las nubes, los árboles, las flores, los pájaros. Hoy, ninguna de esas milagrosas creaciones pasará sin que yo la note.

Hoy, compartiré mi emoción ante la vida con otras personas. Haré sonreir a alguien. Me saldré de lo habitual para realizar un gesto de amabilidad hacia alguien

not even know me. Today I will praise sincerely someone who appears depressed. I will tell a child how special she is and I will tell someone I love how profoundly I care for him and how significant she is to me.

Today is the day when I will let go of my preoccupation for the things that I do not have and be grateful for all the marvelous things that God has already given to me. I will remember that to worry is no more than a waste of time because my faith in God and in God's divine plan assures me that all will end up as it should.

And tonight before I go to bed, I will go out and raise up my eyes to the heavens. I will wonder reverently before the beauty of the stars and the moon and I will praise God for these magnificent treasures.

When the day is finished and my head rests on the pillow, I will give thanks to the Almighty One for the

quien ni sequiera me conoce. Hoy, elogiaré sinceramente a alguien que está depremido. Le diré a una niña que ella es especial y a otros a quien amo lo mucho que significan para mí.

Hoy es el día cuando dejo de preocuparme por lo que no tengo y empiezo a agradecer todas las cosas maravillosas que Dios me ha dado. Recordaré que preocuparse no es más que una pérdida de tiempo porque mi fe en El y en su plan divino me asegura que todo saldrá como debe ser.

Y esta noche, antes de acostarme saldré y levantaré los ojos al cielo. Me asombraré reverente ante la belleza de las estrellas y la luna, y alabaré a Dios por esos magnificos tesoros.

Cuando el día se acabe y mi cabeza repose en la almohada, le daré gracias al Todopoderoso por el mejor día de mi vida. Y dormiré el sueño de un niño satisfecho emocionado con la expectativa,

best day of my life. And I
will sleep the dreams of a
child, satisfied and excited
with the expectation that
tomorrow will be the best
day of my life.

porque se que mañana será
el mejor día en mi vida.

> *Colleen Kammer, Miamisburg, Ohio,*
> *a friend of Maryknoll, a prayer*
> *of an 80-year-old Guatemalan woman,*
> *originally written in Spanish*
> *by Gregory M. Lousing-Nont*

Lord, be the beginning and end of all that I say and do.
Prompt my actions with your grace and complete them
with your all-powerful help. Amen.

> *Monica Z. Greco,*
> *Schenectady, New York,*
> *a friend of Maryknoll*

My God, I offer thee this day,
all I shall think or do or say.
Uniting it with what was done,
on earth by Jesus Christ your Son.

> *Mrs. John Mahoney, Fairfield, Connecticut,*
> *a friend of Maryknoll, from a prayer taught her by*
> *the St. Joseph nuns over sixty years ago*
> *(with a note that it was easier to remember*
> *prayers back when they rhymed)*

Dear Lord,
So far today, God, I've done all right.
I haven't gossiped, haven't lost my temper,
haven't been greedy, grumpy, nasty, selfish, or over-
        indulgent.
I'm really glad about that, but in a few minutes, God,
I'm going to get out of bed, and from then on
I'm probably going to need a lot more help.
Thank you. In Jesus' name. Amen.

Flo Weiss, Breckenridge, Minnesota,
a friend of Maryknoll, author unknown

Prayers for Each Day of the Week

Sunday
I sing a song of praise to you,
Merciful and everlasting God,
Who has given me life and the
Promise of eternal reward. I
Worship you on this day of
Rest, and pray you will watch
Over my friends and family in
The days ahead.

Monday
Dear Jesus, the human family
Is united through the glory of
Your life and resurrection.
Help me to understand that
We are all brothers and sisters
In your eyes. Let me recognize
That we depend upon others.

Grant me humility. Help me
To be generous and kind to
Every life I touch this day.

Tuesday
O source of all creativity,
Open my mind to its fullest.
Let me think and speak with
Wisdom and strength. Guide
My passage through this day
That I use the talents
And skills that you
Generously bestowed upon
Me, in a way that honors
Your holy name.

Wednesday
Lord, sometimes I feel
Battered from all sides.
Afraid and confused, I am
Pulled in opposite directions.
You too were fearful and torn
In the Garden of Gethsemane.
Grant me insight that I
Might choose the path of right
And good. In all things
May your will be done.

Thursday
God, thank you for the gift
Of laughter which eases my
Cares and casts sunshine on
A dark day. As my body

And spirit are lifted and
Tension drops away, let me
See laughter as a reflection
Of your bright light. Today,
Let me enjoy and share your
Joyful gift with everyone
I meet.

Friday
Heavenly Father, you
Embrace us all with the gift
Of your everlasting love.
Yet, this life is not without
Pain, suffering and injustices.
Help me to accept adversity
When it comes my way. Give
Me the courage to overcome
Evil. Hear my prayers for those
Less fortunate than myself.
Grant us peace in the name of
Your son, Savior Jesus.

Saturday
As this week closes, Lord, I
Reflect upon accomplishments
And that which remains
Undone. Help me to count my
Blessings and not dwell upon
Disappointments. Thank you
For being always at my side
And sustaining me through
Ups and downs.

An old Maryknoll prayer booklet

Semana Santan mayisiñatak Jesusan T'aqhisiwipa

A Prayer for Holy Week Jesus' Suffering

1. Alaxpachankir suma
Tatitoxay
Jachkañaw
t'aqhisiwaytaxa. (bis)

1. My good Lord who dwells
in heaven
With great tears you
suffered. (repeat)

Coro:
Cruzana ch'akkatataw
Jumax t'aqhisiwatax
Juchanakax layku jiwtaxa.

Chorus:
Nailed to the cross
You suffered
Because of my sins you died.

Cruzana ch'akkatataw
Jumax loqtasiwatax
Juchanakax layku jiwtaxa.

Nailed to the cross
You offered yourself
Because of my sins you died.

2. Jaqinak qhispiyaña
laykukiway,
Jumax wilam
wartasiwayta. (bis)

2. For the salvation of all
people
You shed your blood.
(repeat)

3. Kunayman jawq'ataw
uñjasiwayta
Aca mundor qhispiyañ
layku. (bis)

3. Totally beaten were you
seen
For the salvation of the
world. (repeat)

4. Janiw kunampis
kutiykirismati,
Chuymaxak loqtasiña
munsma. (bis)

4. Not for anything will I
turn away,
I want to offer you my
heart. (repeat)

*Father Robert Hurteau, M.M., an Aymara (Peru)
prayer for Holy Week. It is often sung slowly
in rural areas using a mixture of monotone
and ascending and descending tones.*

On Holy Saturday

Let me crawl into the Holy Sepulcher with you, my Jesus.
Let me lean my head on your chest.
Let me kiss your wounded brow and each wound in your
    hands, feet and side.
Let me, with the angels, minister to your body: bathing it
    gently, wrapping it with perfumed cloths, position-
    ing it in a restful manner, weeping over your
    precious body—sacrificed for all humankind.
    Smoothing your hair, touching your face, weep-
    ing, weeping, loving you because you first loved
    me.

Marilyn Nowlin, San Antonio, Texas,
a friend of Maryknoll

Prayers for Each Month

January
Lord of Heaven, in
Your infinite wisdom
And mercy you have granted me
A new year, another chance to
Turn to you and find happiness
And peace.

Look upon all who have yet to
Hear your name or experience
Your compassion, and grant that
We all may discover you anew in
Everyone we meet today.

Father Joseph Veneroso, M.M.,
Maryknoll, New York

February
Heavenly Father,
Source of all love,
You gave me love in your Son,
Jesus Christ. He taught me love
By his life and death; help me
To imitate the divine example.

Let me reflect your love in my
Family, with friends and
Associates. Let me forgive
Quickly when hurt; be gentle
When angry.

Grant me peace in your love,
Knowing that my quest for love
Will find fulfillment only when I
Rest in thee.

Friend of the Missions

March
Spirit of the living God
Fall afresh on us.

Free us, heal us,
Empower us to love
Others as you love them.

Draw us to the wellspring
Of all life—communion with
Jesus the Lord.

Father Joseph Veneroso, M.M.,
Maryknoll, New York

April
Lord, as the day's light
Lingers longer in the
Heavens, and all your creatures
Turn expectantly toward spring,
Help me to renew my life, as
You renew nature.

Give me the courage to look at
My imperfections. Give me the
Courage to change that which
Does not honor thee.

Let me sing your praise for the
Wonder of the world you have
Given us. And let me seek ever to
Make it better in your name.

Jackie Ring

May
Mary, heavenly mother,
Thank you for protecting
All your earthly children in the
Shelter of your mantle.

For showing me a mother's love
And embracing me despite my
Shortcomings. For helping me
To stand again when I stumble
And fall.

I pray that you will take my
Hand and guide me forward in

Love and service to your son,
Our Lord, Jesus Christ.

A Maryknoll Lay Associate

June
Savior Jesus, you have
Given all humankind
The ultimate opportunity for
Redemption through your life
And death. You showed us the
Path through your teachings.

Help me to strive daily toward
The fulfillment of your promise,
As I take each new step in life,
Let me do it in your image and
With your blessing.

Help me to not falter, nor be
Afraid of failure, knowing that I
Must risk to gain the kingdom of
Heaven and that if you are with
Me, I cannot fail.

A friend of Maryknoll

July
Lord Jesus, it was you
Who first taught that all
People are created equal. That we
Are endowed by you with certain
Inalienable rights to life, liberty
And the pursuit of happiness.

Thank you for the privilege of
Being an American, for living in
A country founded on your
Principles, for the freedom to
Freely worship you, my God.

When we fail as a people to do
Your will, grant all our leaders
Wisdom, that they might guide
Us back to a godly path.
God, please bless America.

Jackie Ring

August
God, I see children
Playing by the sea and both
Speak to me of your almighty
Power.

You created the little ones from
Small seeds. You breathed life
Into their souls. You made them
In your image. The sea, too, is
Your child, your creation which
Sustains humankind and the
Animals here below.

Both child and sea can be kind,
And again, merciless. Let me
Rest content, knowing that in
Your wisdom, all will be done
According to your divine will.

Anonymous

September
The world may be the
Only classroom most
Children have; adults,
Their only textbook.

And what they see and hear
And learn along the way will
Shape their thoughts, color their
Words and season their actions.

Each unselfish act of kindness,
Justice and compassion echoes
The teachings of Christ.

Go, therefore, make disciples of
All nations, you who have
Learned from childhood what
"Our Father" means.

Father Joseph Veneroso, M.M.,
Maryknoll, New York

October
Lord, make me an instrument of your peace;
Where there is hatred, let me sow
Love; where there is injury,
Pardon; where there is doubt,
Faith; where there is despair, hope;
Where there is darkness, light;
And where there is sadness, joy.

O Divine Master, grant that I may
Not so much seek to be consoled

As to console, to be understood
As to understand, to be loved as
To love.

For it is in giving that we receive;
It is in pardoning that we are
Pardoned; and it is dying that
We are born to eternal life.

Attributed to St. Francis of Assisi

November
My heart turns to you,
O Lord, in this season
Of Thanksgiving; all I am and
Hope to be is directed by your
Almighty vision. All I have or
Hope to find is dependent upon
Your divine mercy. I offer you
My heart, as I offer you my
Thanks, for all you have granted
Me through your everlasting love.

A Maryknoll Missioner

December
Baby Jesus, I see you
In the manger there;
Tiny, fragile, wispy hair.
You look upon your mother's face.
Does she know you've come to
    Save the race?
I think of babies that I've known,

And how each has quickly grown
To heights their mothers never
    Dreamed.
To your mother, too, I'm sure it
    Seemed
You'd always be a baby fair.
Keep me in your loving care,
Baby Jesus, Savior Jesus.

An anonymous Maryknoll Affiliate

A Prayer for Good Health and for Community

I give you thanks, Lord, for keeping in good health all my family and all my brothers and sisters in Christ. I thank you for the rain you send for our crops and for giving us our daily bread.

I also pray for my children, so they may do well in their studies and that they may advance, because we can only do well with your power and blessing.

I also pray for the sick in our community. They are faithful to you, Lord, but because of their illness they cannot join us in prayer. May you heal them, Lord, so they can be with us as brothers and sisters united in your house of prayer.

Also, I want to pray for all those brothers and sisters who don't come to your church. May you touch their hearts so they may come closer to your church. I thank you, Lord!

Sister Joan Uhlen, M.M., Chacraseca,
Nicaragua, a prayer of Amanda Mendez
(translated by Sister Bernice Kita, M.M.)

Slow Me Down, Lord

Slow me down, Lord. Ease the pounding of my heart by the quieting of my mind. Steady my hurried pace with a vision of the eternal reach of time. Give me, amid the confusion of the day, the calmness of the everlasting hills. Break the tensions of my nerves and muscles with the soothing music of the singing streams that live in my memory.

Help me to know the magical, restoring power of sleep. Teach me the art of taking minute vacations—of slowing down to look at a flower, to chat with a friend, to pat a dog, to read a few lines from a good book.

Slow me down, Lord, and inspire me to send my roots deep into the soil of life's enduring values that I may grow toward the stars of my greater destiny.

E. P. Hughes, Ishpeming, Michigan,
a friend of Maryknoll, author unknown

Dear Jesus,
I love you, so help me today.
Make me a little stronger each and every day.
Take away my big pains,
little ones can stay.
I know I must suffer for the sins I have made.
Forgive me, sweet Jesus, as I go on my way.
Love everlasting, Amen, I pray.

Irene Czech, Holdingford, Minnesota,
a friend of Maryknoll

Come to me, sweet Jesus, come to me and stay,
for I love you, Jesus, more than I can say.
Mary, keep Jesus in my heart, our Lady, our Queen, our
    Mother.
In the name of Jesus and for the love of Jesus, I implore
    thee,
take this cause in thy hands, and grant me good success.
St. Joseph, friend of the sacred heart, pray for us.

Eileen M. Hanley, Lindstrom, Minnesota,
a long-time supporter of Maryknoll,
from a prayer of Sister Timothea, learned
in sixth grade and taught to children,
grandchildren, and great-grandchildren

Prayer of St. Ephrem

O Lord and Master of my life,
keep from me the spirit of indifference and discourage-
    ment,
lust of power, and idle chatter.

Instead, grant to me, your servant,
the spirit of wholeness of being, humble-mindedness, pa-
    tience, and love.

O Lord and King,
grant me the grace to be aware of my sins
and not to judge others;
for you are blessed now and forever. Amen.

Dorothy Hleba, West Mifflin, Pennsylvania,
a Byzantine Catholic friend of Maryknoll

Carry me through today, Lord,
With your gentle wings from above.
Carry me through today, Lord.
Let me feel your love.
I shall not worry about tomorrow;
Yesterday is gone.
Just carry me through today, Lord;
That's where I belong.
Through all my trials and troubles,
I know that you are there:
Sometimes it's hard to see you,
Through each tear and care.
Carry me through today, Lord;
Don't let me slip away.
Tomorrow may be taken from me,
So carry me through today. . . .

Jo Bryant, Floydada, Texas,
a friend of Maryknoll

O Lord, support us all the day long of this troubled life, until the shadows lengthen and evening comes and the busy world is hushed and the fever of life is over and our work is done. Then of Thy great mercy grant us a safe lodging and a holy rest and peace at the last, through Jesus Christ, our Lord. Amen.

Alice Gould, Staten Island, New York,
a friend of Maryknoll,
from a prayer card for her nephew Neil Dollard,
who was killed at the World Trade Center
on September 11, 2001

Prayer of Daily Intentions

Lord, grant that I may meet with spiritual peace all that this day will bring to me. Grant that I may wholeheartedly submit myself to your will. Whatever news I receive today, teach me to accept it with a peaceful soul and with a firm conviction that, in all things, your holy will will be done. In all my words and deeds, guide my thoughts and feelings. Teach me to deal with all people in a simple and wise manner without offending or saddening anyone.

Lord, grant to me the strength to endure the weariness and all the situations of this day. Guide my will and teach me to pray, to believe, to hope, to endure, forgive, and love.

Alice Kubin, Whiting, New Jersey,
a friend of Maryknoll

O Lord, King of the Universe, bestow on us your children the image of faith, hope, and charity among all people of the world. Give us the grace to overcome obstacles that we encounter in life. We offer all sacrifices for the greater honor and glory of God who lives and reigns forever and ever. Amen.

Lucile V. Garcia, Brooklyn, New York,
a friend of Maryknoll

"Do not think that the words of prayer as you say them go up to God. It is not the words themselves that ascend; it is rather the burning desire of your heart that rises like smoke toward heaven."

⚓ *Marianne K. Lowe and Janice M. Lowe,*
Parma, Ohio, friends of Maryknoll,
from a Hasidic saying

Michael's Prayer: A Prayer for Travelers

I feel grateful for having this choice to be here with the
family.
I thank God for bringing me here safely.
I thank God for all the people who kept me in their prayers.
I ask God to bless those people tonight with a restful sleep
and sweet dreams of hope.
No more can be said; a featherbed awaits me.

*MaryAnne Greyerbiehl, Saginaw, Michigan,
mother of Maryknoll Brother Michael Greyerbiehl,
a prayer from his diary (Brother Michael died in
2001 at age 38 while on mission in Japan)*

Before Reading the Bible

Come, Lord Jesus, come.
Our Lord Jesus Christ, you are the Word of the Father.
You became one with us to tell us of the Father's love.
You are the light that shines in the darkness.
You save us from fear and break the bonds of sin and death.
You come to guide our steps and lead us to God.
You are the Word of eternal life.
You fill us with the Holy Spirit.

After Reading the Bible

We have heard your words, Jesus.
They give us joy and bring light and truth into our lives.
Your presence gives us peace in our troubled and divided
world.

Let your Word create in our hearts a deep desire for you.
Be with us in our hearts and home, in our community and
       our country.
Give us your Holy Spirit to help us to understand your
       Word.
We enthrone now this Holy Bible in our midst.
Make your Word the center of our lives.
May your Word inspire all that we think and say and do.
May your Word bind us together in unity with each other
       and with you.
Today and forever. Amen.

Prayers from Paulines Publications,
Nairobi, Kenya

Come, Holy Ghost, Creator Blest,
And in my heart,
Take up thy rest,
Come with thy grace and heavenly aid
To fill the hearts that thou has made. Amen.

Kathy Crann, Brielle, New Jersey,
a friend of Maryknoll,
traditional hymn

Angel of God, my guardian dear,
To whom God's love commits me here,
   Ever this day be at my side,
To light and guard, to rule and guide. Amen.

Mary Luniewski, Richmond Hill, New York,
a friend of Maryknoll,
traditional prayer

A Prayer after Communion

Lord Jesus, I give you my will that you may penetrate it with your energies. I give you my mind that you may fill it with your thoughts.

Take my talents, Jesus, and my gifts and help me to develop them for your honor and glory.

I give you my weaknesses that you might strengthen me. How much I need you, Lord!

I give you my heart. Please fill it with your love.

I give you all my sinfulness, my selfishness. Have mercy on me, Lord!

I cast all my cares, my worries, my concerns on you, Lord. I know that you care about me and that you will help me always.

Lord Jesus, I give you all of me. Take me and do with me as it pleases you. Make me more like you, more pleasing to the Father, more open to the work of the Holy Spirit.

Thank you for giving me yourself in this Eucharist!

William and Marilyn Bernhard, Bancroft, Iowa,
friends of Maryknoll

Though I am old, my heart sings,
Sweet promises of coming spring,
The magic of a bright, full moon,
Swaying cattails on the dune,
The rising and setting of the glorious sun,
Dear God, let this be until my day is done.

Mary Burke, Staten Island, New York,
a friend of Maryknoll

A Small Prayer

Jesus, meek and humble of heart,
Make our hearts like unto Thine.

Eva Caruso, Akron, Ohio,
a friend of Maryknoll,
traditional prayer

A Prayer for Children

Jesus, tender shepherd, hear me.
Bless thy little child tonight.
Through the darkness be thou near me,
Keep me safe till morning light.
All the day thy hand has led me
And I thank thee for thy care.
Thou hast warmed and clothed and fed me,
Listen to my evening prayer.
Keep me now from every danger,
Let thy angel guard my bed.
Thou hast nothing but a manger
Where to lay thy infant head.
Let my sins be all forgiven,
Bless the friends I love so well.
Take me when I die to heaven
Happy there with thee to dwell.
Now I close my eyes so weary,
Fold my arms upon my breast,
Praying thee my God to bless me
As I gently sink to rest.

Lucille Jiambalvo, Lemont, Illinois,
a friend of Maryknoll,
a prayer she learned
as a child some eighty years ago

A Prayer for Children for First Communion

You have come to my heart, dearest Jesus,
I'm holding you close to my breast,
I'm telling you over and over,
You are welcome, my Little White Guest.

I love you, I love you, my Jesus,
O, please do not think I am bold,
Of course you must know that I love you,
But I'm sure that you like to be told.

And when I shall meet you in heaven,
My head will then lean on your breast,
and you will recall our fond meetings,
When you were my Little White Guest.

Velma Espinoza, Denver, Colorado,
a Maryknoll partner in mission since 1957,
a prayer she learned for her First Communion
fifty-five years ago

Little Jesus come to me,
Make a good child out of me.
My heart is small
No room at all
Except for thee
My little Jesus. Amen.

Lenara Tuchmann Boyd, Gordon, Texas,
a friend of Maryknoll,
from a prayer she learned from
her grandparents who emigrated from Germany
in the 1840s, taught to her nine children,
and still finds consoling at age 87

In these moments, Lord,
I empty my hands and open them to you.
I let go of anger; fill and bless me with your love.
I let go of guilt; fill and bless me with forgiveness.
I let go of self-pity; fill and bless me with a grateful heart.
I let go of worries and fear; fill and bless me with trust.
I let go of the hurts of the past; fill and bless me with the
      promise of the present.

Bless me and keep me, Lord.
Let your face shine upon me, uphold me, and give me
      peace.

*Jeanne L. Klein, Toledo, Ohio, from a prayer
of Fay Angus* (Daily Guideposts, *2002)*

Take my hand, O Blessed Mother.
Hold me firmly lest I fall.
I am nervous when I am walking.
On you I humbly call.
Guide me over crossings.
Watch me when I'm on the stairs.
Let me know you're beside me.
Listen to my reverent prayer.
Bring me to my destination safely,
Every single day.
When night falls upon us,
And I fear to be alone,
Take my hand, O Blessed Mother,
Protect me and my home.

*Ann Kaider, Bella Vista, Arizona,
a friend of Maryknoll,
author unknown*

My day is ending and I give thanks to you, O Lord. Evening is at hand, furnish it with brightness. As day has its evening, so also does life. The evening of life is age and age has overtaken me. Furnish it with brightness. Do not cast me aside in my time of age. Do not forsake me as my strength fails. Abide in me, Lord, and let your strength be made perfect in my weakness.

Doris V. Monteil, Kansas City, Missouri,
a friend of Maryknoll, a prayer of Bishop Lancelot
Andrewes (seventeenth century)

The Evening Has Fallen

Now that evening has fallen,
To God, the Creator, I will turn in prayer,
Knowing that he will help me.
I know the Father will help me.

John Mbiti, Kenya, from a prayer of the Dinka of
Sudan from The Prayers of African Religion
(Orbis Books, 1975)

A Prayer When Visiting Another

O Lord God, I praise and thank you for the wonderful and awesome gift of life and for your abiding presence with me. Be with me today as I visit *(names)* and bring them your good news. O God, I thank you for the precious gifts of these people. May I brighten their day, give them a sense of being remembered, and take the time to listen to their needs and concerns. Give them comfort in their daily crosses, in their times of loneliness, and in their regrets of what they have or have not done. May your peace, O Lord, surround them and cause them to be filled with your love and to lift their hearts in joyful hope to you. Amen.

Brother Kevin Brutcher, FSC, Fridley, Minnesota,
a friend of Maryknoll

Jesus, help me for a few moments tonight to be still and silent in mind, body and spirit, so that I might hear and take to heart the words faith tells me the heavenly Father whispers to me constantly: "You are my beloved." Amen.

Joan K. Karter, Buffalo, New York,
a friend of Maryknoll,
from a "Living Faith" devotional booklet

Good Night, O Lord

Before I go to sleep, O Lord, I want to say this prayer,
That you will always keep me in your kind and loving care,
That you will let my body rest and let my mind relax,
And fill my dreams with holy thoughts instead of worldly
      facts.
I ask that you forgive me for my failures of today,
And give me all the grace I need to live a better way.
Watch over me tonight, O Lord, and in my heart instill
The fervor and the constancy to do your holy will.
I want to follow you and grow more worthy in your sight.
O Lord, please listen to my prayer and hear me say good
      night.

Leo Halfpenny, Northville, Michigan,
a friend of Maryknoll

Prayer at the End of the Day

At the end of the day we praise you, Lord.
We thank you for the graces that have come to us this day
      from your hands.
For bringing us safely through this day, we thank you.
For the work you have given us, we thank you.
For the food you have given us to eat, we thank you.
For all we have learned and received from others, we thank
      you.
Forgive us the faults we committed this day.
For our laziness, our neglect of others, our want of love,
Lord, we are truly sorry.
Pour out your blessings on our family.
May we be one as you are one.
In generosity and love we forgive and ask forgiveness this
      night
for any sharp word we spoke today
or anything we did in anger or in haste.
We remember those who have died.
Grant them eternal rest.
We pray for the whole world—
the sick, the lonely and all who suffer injustice.
Lord, help us to help them.
Visit, O Lord, this house.
Keep it safe from all hatred and danger.
Protect our property.
May your holy angels keep us in peace
and may your blessings be always upon us.
Through Jesus your Son, our Lord
who lives and reigns with you and the Holy Spirit,
forever and ever. Amen.

Susie Giannoni, Maryknoll Sisters, New York,
from prayers from Derry, Northern Ireland

Eventide

As the soft shadows of
Twilight play across the
Sky, I thank you, almighty
Father, for bringing me safely
Through another day.

I have tried to do your will and
I pray you will look kindly upon
My efforts. I will rest now, relax
My burdens and enjoy these
Waning hours.

Please grant me refreshing sleep
And the blessing of a new dawn.

A Maryknoll Missioner

Lord of night, Creator of the stars and the moon,
I thank you for the graceful gifts of this day.
I rest in Thee, my Divine Friend and Companion,
who watches over me while I sleep.
May the problems and pains of today
be healed as I surrender myself to your nightly care.
Bless those whom I love and for whom I have promised to
     pray,
and watch over them in a special way.

Lord of day and night, of life and death,
I place myself into your holy hands. Amen.

Patricia A. Rolewicz,
Mendota Heights, Minnesota,
a friend of Maryknoll

Night Prayer

Angel of God, my guardian dear,
To whom God's love commits me here,
Ever this night be at my side
To light and guard,
To rule and guide.
From sinful stain
Oh, keep me free;
In the hour of my death
My comfort be.

Frances Lange, Brooklyn Center, Minnesota,
a friend of Maryknoll,
traditional prayer

Evening Prayer of St. Augustine

Watch thou, O Lord, with those who wake, or watch, or
weep tonight,
and give thine angels and saints charge over those who
sleep.
Tend thy sick ones, O Lord Jesus Christ.
Rest thy weary ones,
Bless thy dying ones,
Soothe thy suffering ones,
Pity thy afflicted ones,
Shield thy joyous ones,
And all for thy love's sake. Amen.

Elizabeth Sokolowski, Sioux City, Iowa,
a friend of Maryknoll

A Healing Prayer at Bedtime
for September 11, 2001

Jesus, through the power of the Holy Spirit,
go back into my memory as I sleep.
Every hurt that has ever been done to me, heal that hurt.
Every hurt that I have ever caused to another person, heal
      that hurt.
All the relationships that have been damaged in my whole
      life that I am not aware of, heal those relation-
      ships.
But, Lord, if there is anything that I need to do,
if I need to go to a person because he is still suffering from
      my hand,
bring to my awareness that person.
I choose to forgive and I ask to be forgiven.
Remove whatever bitterness may be in my heart, Lord,
and fill the empty spaces with your love.
Thank you, Jesus. Amen.

Mary Brady, Seal Beach, California,
a friend of Maryknoll,
a prayer of the Oblate Missions

Mary and the Saints

"He has looked with favor on the lowliness of his servant. Surely, from now on all generations will call me blessed; for the Mighty One has done great things for me, and holy is his name."

LUKE 1:48–49

Likewise the Spirit helps us in our weakness; for we do not know how to pray as we ought, but that very Spirit intercedes. . . . And God, who searches the heart, knows what is the mind of the Spirit, because the Spirit intercedes for the saints according to the will of God.

ROMANS 8:26–27

John and Paul (the Beatles, not the Apostles) got it right: "We get by with a little help from our friends" (the Apostles would agree).

We have friends on earth and friends in heaven. Mary, Joseph, and the saints help us get through life by their example and intercession. Praying with them is an ancient tradition. Need a little help? Let us pray.

☙

Mary Most Holy, Mother of All Nations,
help us remember
that the universe is all one song of praise
and we are all created to be the beloved of God.
Make us all one in the Trinity.
All nations. No nations.
No boundaries, only expanses.
No borders, only homelands
No separations, only communion.
As it was in the beginning. Amen.

Megan McKenna,
from Mary, Mother of All Nations
(Orbis Books, 2000)

Dear Mother Mary, at the Cana wedding, the simple statement from you, "There is no more wine," prompted Jesus to perform his first miracle, changing water into rich wine.

Mother, you know all the troublesome situations in our families, our country, and in the world today. Our supply of tolerance of each other, our charity, sacrifice, and love of peace are running low. We honor you in our rosary and we implore you to ask God, through your Son, Jesus, to forgive us our frailties and to change into rich substance that in our hearts which has become weak, watery, and shallow.

Virginia S. Adamowicz,
Nashua, New Hampshire,
a friend of Maryknoll

The Magnificat

My soul doth magnify the Lord,
and my spirit rejoices in God my Savior.
For he has regarded the low estate of his handmaiden.
For behold, henceforth all generations will call me blessed;
for he who is mighty has done great things for me,
and holy is his name.
And his mercy is on those who fear him
from generation to generation.
He has shown strength with his arm,
he has scattered the proud in their conceit,
he has cast down the mighty from their thrones,
and has lifted up the lowly;
he has filled the hungry with good things,
and the rich he has sent away empty.
He has helped his servant Israel,
in remembrance of his mercy,
as he spoke to our fathers,
to Abraham and his children for ever.

Ruth E. Matthews, Bethel Park, Pennsylvania,
a friend of Maryknoll
(Luke 1:47–55)

Our Lady of Maryknoll, we ask you to help us understand that wherever there is suffering, there, too, is your son's loving hand. He is there in the touch of a missioner, in the smile of a new friend. He is there in the prayer of a stranger, in our faith that knows no end. Dear Mary, walk beside us and help us realize that we can ease another's pain. We can put hope in a child's eyes.

From a prayer card
of the Maryknoll Fathers and Brothers

Dulce Madre	Sweet Mother
Dulce Madre, no te alejes.	Sweet Mother, do not depart from me.
Tu vista de mi no apartes.	
Ven conmigo a todas partes,	Do not lose me from your sight.
y solo(a) nunca me dejes.	
Ya que me proteges tanto,	Accompany me everywhere
como verdadera Madre,	and never leave me all alone.
haz que me bendiga el Padre,	Because you protect me like a true Mother,
el Hijo, y el Espíritu Santo.	obtain for me the blessing of the Father,
Amén.	the Son, and the Holy Spirit. Amen.

Eileen M. Mulhare, Hamilton, New York,
from a popular prayer from Mexico

Memorare

Remember, O most gracious Virgin Mary,
that never was it known that anyone who fled to thy protection,
implored thy help, or sought thy intercession,
was left unaided.
Inspired with this confidence,
I fly unto thee, O Virgin of virgins, my Mother.
To thee I come, before thee I stand,
sinful and sorrowful.
O Mother of the Word Incarnate,
despise not my petitions,
but in thy clemency hear and answer me. Amen.

Bishop William J. McNaughton, M.M., Inchon, Korea,
from Maryknoll Fathers' Prayer Book (1963)

Prayer for Peace to Mary
of the Immaculate Conception

Mary Immaculate,
Patroness of the United States,
we praise and thank God
for the many blessings showered upon our land.

We ask you to intercede for us now,
that we as a people of God
may learn to live true justice and peace
with all people.

We ask that the whole world community
will come to share the same rich blessings.

We pray especially for our leaders:
with wisdom, fortitude and compassion,
may they guide our nation away from all terrorism.

We ask this, Mary,
in the name of the Father,
and of your Son, Jesus,
and through the power of the Holy Spirit. Amen.

Margaret E. Homan, Milton, Wisconsin,
a friend of Maryknoll,
a prayer of Mary Therese Gallagher

Hail Mary, full of grace.
The Lord is with you.
Blessed are you among women,
and blessed is the fruit of your womb, Jesus.
Holy Mary, Mother of God, pray for us sinners,
now and at the hour of our death. Amen.

Father Paul O'Brien, M.M., La Paz, Bolivia,
traditional prayer

Hail, Holy Queen

Hail, holy queen, Mother of Mercy, our life, our sweet-
ness and our hope!
To thee do we cry, poor banished children of Eve,
To thee do we send up our sighs, mourning and weeping
in this valley of tears,
Turn then, most gracious advocate, thine eyes of mercy
toward us,
And after this, our exile, show to us the blessed fruit of thy
womb, Jesus.
O clement, O loving, O sweet Virgin Mary,
Pray for us, O Holy Mother of God,
That we may be made worthy of the promises of Christ.

*Edward Hayde, Mission Promotion,
Maryknoll, New York, traditional prayer*

Night is falling, dear Mother, the long day is o'er,
And before your loved image, I'm kneeling once more,
To thank you for keeping me safe through the day,
To ask you this night to keep evil away.

I'm going to rest, for the day's work is done,
Its hours and moments have passed, one by one,
And the God who will judge me has counted them all,
He has numbered each grace, He has counted each fall.

And if e'er the dawn I should draw my last breath,
And the sleep that I take be the long sleep of death,
Be near me, dear Mother, for Jesus' dear sake,
When my soul on eternity's shore shall awake.

*Mary C. Vittengl, Lake George, New York,
a friend of Maryknoll*

Born in a Cave to a Woman Named Mary

María Elba fled her house in northern El Salvador and went into the mountains. Under constant air bombardments, she became separated from her husband. During this time she hid in a cave and at night, when she was alone, her son Alex was born. She cut his umbilical cord with a stone and the following day continued her journey toward the Honduran border. Six days later she arrived at the Lempa River, which separates El Salvador and Honduras. She wrapped six-day-old Alex in a shirt and placed him in a large, empty sack. Under a constant bombardment, María Elba swam across the river, holding on tight to that sack, and made it to safety in Honduras.

O Blessed Mary, you were not the only one who was denied a room. So was I, when my son was born on a mountain, naked, without swaddling clothes. Only you, Blessed Virgin, accompanied me when my son was born in the dark, when I was alone on that dark mountain, because we were fleeing from El Salvador.

O God and Blessed Mary, help us return to our country, El Salvador. I am a young woman who has suffered much. I have spent many nights fleeing in the rain, just like you, Blessed Virgin, who fled with your son. My parents, brothers and sisters have also suffered much, just like you, who suffered with your son.

Father Paul Belliveau, M.M.,
San Pedro Sula, Honduras

O Virgin Mary,
servant of God and of women and men
in saying "yes" to the angel of God
and to God's plan of justice and liberation,
hear us.

Mary, you were scorned when seeking room in Bethlehem.
You were rejected when your son, Jesus, was born in a
          manger.
You were persecuted when you fled your country.
Virgin Mary, since you experienced all these sufferings,
we ask you also to give us resistance and courage for our
          journey.
Do not allow us to lose heart during the pilgrimage,
for you, my mother, suffered the same sufferings we suffer.

Father Paul Belliveau, M.M.,
San Pedro Sula, Honduras,
from a prayer of an El Salvadoran
refugee woman

O Mary, our Lady of Africa, whose stainless heart is full
of mercy and maternal compassion, by your loving intercession, obtain for the peoples of Africa knowledge and
love of Christ, in order to serve him faithfully. May a growing charity and a spirit of unity free them from present
dangers and draw them closer to union with all humankind through the redeeming blood of your Son, Jesus
Christ, our Lord. Amen.

Sister Barbara Hendricks, M.M.,
Maryknoll, New York, from a prayer
of Mother Mary Joseph Rogers,
foundress of the Maryknoll Sisters

Prayer to Our Lady of Fatima

I greet you, Queen of the Heavens,
on this day with great love,
asking you to be the mother of the orphan who has no
  home.
In silence, suffering and crying out for your motherly protection,
you, Mary, raised your arms and covered me with your
  love.

To you come all the wandering children of the world.
O Blessed Mother, give us your hand;
you who have suffered just like me.
O Beloved Mother, all we children sing together with great
  fervor
and give you thanks for being the Mother of the poor.
We pray that you will grant peace to the world.

Father Paul Belliveau, M.M.,
San Pedro Sula, Honduras, from prayers
of refugee Salvadoran children
on the Feast of Our Lady of Fatima

O Mother of Perpetual Help

O Mother of Perpetual Help, grant that I may ever in-
voke thy most powerful name, which is the safeguard of
the living and the salvation of the dying. O purest Mary,
O sweetest Mary, let thy name henceforth be ever on my
lips. Delay not, O Blessed Lady, to help me, whenever I call
on thee; for in all my temptations, in all my needs, I shall
never cease to call on thee, ever repeating thy sacred name,
Mary, Mary. Oh, what consolation, what sweetness, what

confidence, what emotion fill my soul when I utter thy sacred name, or even only think of thee.

I thank the Lord for having given thee, for my good, so sweet, so powerful, so lovely a name. But I will not be content with merely uttering thy name. Let my love for thee prompt me ever to hail thee, Mother of Perpetual Help. Obtain for me, therefore, the pardon of my sins, love for Jesus, final perseverance, and the grace ever to have recourse to thee, O Mother of Perpetual Help.

Ann Wilson, Ferndale, Michigan, a Maryknoll supporter for thirty-five years (now 84, Ann learned this prayer when she made her first Holy Communion at age 8)

A Missioner's Prayer

O Mary, Mother of Good Counsel, intercede for us who work in the missionary field. Keep us under thy protection and care as we seek to counsel the young, comfort the afflicted, give courage to the downtrodden. Teach us the kindness and gentleness of the heart of your Divine Son when He suffered little children to come to Him; inspire us with the wisdom, understanding and fortitude of the Holy Spirit.

Help us to assist those who place their trust in us, that we may point the way to peace and happiness here on earth, and eternally in heaven. Guide us all, dear Lady, along the paths leading to the Heavenly Kingdom where you await us in the company of your loving Son.

Rosemary P. Lamoureux, West Melbourne, Florida, a friend of Maryknoll

Prayer to Our Blessed Mother
of the Elderly and Infirm

Take my hand, O blessed Mother,
Hold me firmly, lest I fall.
I grow nervous while I'm walking and on thee I humbly
    call.
Guide me over every crossing,
Watch me when I'm on the stairs.
Let me know that you're beside me,
Listen to my fervent prayers.
Bring me to my destination safely along the way.
Bless my every undertaking and my duties for the day.
And when evening creeps upon us and I fear to be alone,
Once again, O blessed Mother, take my hand and lead me
    home.

*Irene Herley, West Chester, Pennsylvania,
a friend of Maryknoll (This beautiful prayer
for the aging and infirm was sent in
by many people.)*

Act of Consecration
to the Immaculate Heart of Mary

To your Immaculate Heart, dear Mary, our Sovereign
Queen, we lovingly consecrate our community, its members and its goods throughout the world to be used by you
in whatever way is in accord with the adorable will and
good pleasure of Jesus. We ask only that you show us the
way and guide us on to the end.

We hope through this consecration to aid in bringing
peace to the world and in drawing all to know, love and

serve God to the end that all things may be restored in Christ. We trust, too, dear Blessed Mother, that it rightly expresses our devoted love to you, our filial confidence in you, and our will to have all things go to Jesus through your Immaculate Heart.

Sister Barbara Hendricks, M.M.,
Maryknoll, New York, from a prayer
of Mother Mary Joseph Rogers,
foundress of the Maryknoll Sisters

I love thee, O Mary, with all
the love of the Eternal Father
who has created thee so lovely.
I love thee, O Mary, with all
the love of the Word
who became incarnate in thy bosom.

I love thee, O Mary, with all
the love of the Holy Spirit
whose temple thou hast become.
I love thee, O Mary, with all
the love of the angels and saints,
with all the love of St. Joachim and St. Anne,
St. Joseph and St. John.

In all the places of the earth where a soul tells
thee she loves thee
I unite myself to this soul, O Mary,
and to all the Ave Marias that
shall be said in the entire universe. Amen!

Sister Mariel Vitcavage, M.M.,
Maryknoll, New York

To Our Lady

Lovely Lady dressed in blue—
Teach me how to pray.
God was just your little boy,
Tell me what to say.

Did you lift him up, sometimes,
Gently on your knee?
Did you sing to him the way
Mother does to me?

Did you hold his hand at night?
Did you ever try
Telling stories of the world?
Oh, and did he cry?

Do you really think he cares
If I tell him things—
Little things that happen? And
Do the angels' wings
Make a noise? And can he hear
Me if I speak low?
Does he understand me now?
Tell me—for you know.

Lovely Lady dressed in blue,
Teach me how to pray.
God was just your little boy,
and you know the way.

Barbara Wisdom, Hollis, New York,
a friend of Maryknoll,
author unknown

Prayer for Parishes

Most glorious Virgin Mary, chosen by the Father to be mother of His Son, known for your purity, for your compassionate heart, for your love, we beseech you to intercede for us in our time of need.

We, at *(name of parish)*, ask your guidance and counsel to strengthen the fabric of our parish that we may be united in our efforts to revitalize our Christian faith. Help us to make our parish a true example of Catholic family living—young and mature, working together to grow in God's image. Amen.

(As a closing to our gatherings, we give thanks to Mary and pray that we can continue to grow in God's image.)

Thank you, Mary, for being with us through this time of gathering. Please stay with each of us that we may keep good feelings, enthusiasm and purpose in our lives. Please help us to encourage devotion to you, Mary, by our good example and prayers. Amen.

Barbara D. Morris, Bolivar, New York,
a friend of Maryknoll

Blessed Joseph, guide our missioners in all lands
as you guided into Egypt Mary and her divine Son.
Help them to sustain with patience trials of soul and weariness of body.
Secure for them abundant grace,
and whatever material aid they may need
to set up tabernacles for Jesus among those who know him not.

From the Maryknoll Sisters' Prayer Book
(1965)

This prayer may be used in the morning before families leave for school or work to keep minds and wills fastened to the Eternal, unencumbered by earthly concerns, reminded of the need for humility, and ready to do the will of God.

May Mary wrap you in the mantle of her protection.

May St. Michael and St. Benedict protect you from all evil and all harm.

May St. Joseph and the Holy Spirit assist you with all your work—

mental, physical, and spiritual.

May God the Father and God the Son surround you with their love,

and fill you with love for others, and others with love for you,

and may you feel my love all day long.

And may Saint *(name your loved one's guardian angel)* safekeep you.

In the name of the Father, and of the Son, and of the Holy Spirit. Amen.

*Kim P. Catalano, Charlotte, North Carolina,
a friend of Maryknoll*

Prayer to St. Joseph

St. Joseph, you are that faithful and wise servant, who by divine providence was the guardian and protector of the life of Jesus. You were the support and consolation of Mary, the Mother of Jesus, and her faithful associate in the plan of our redemption. Yours, O Joseph, was the happiness of living in the company of Jesus and Mary as the chaste spouse of the Mother of God.

We thank God for the favors he bestowed on you. May we imitate the virtues you demonstrated in life here on earth. Watch over us, as we move forward with this project *(name project)*. By your prayers for us and by our intercessions may we be united in mind and heart in the months ahead. Whatever we do, may it be for the greater honor and glory of God. St. Joseph, pray for us.

Father John F. Cain, Sioux Rapids, Iowa,
a friend of Maryknoll

Prayer to St. Anthony

O holy St. Anthony, gentlest of saints, your love for God and charity for God's creatures made you worthy, when on earth, to possess miraculous powers. Encouraged by this thought, I implore you to obtain for me *(request)*.

O gentle and loving St. Anthony, whose heart was ever full of human sympathy, whisper my petition into the ears of the sweet infant Jesus, who loved to be folded in your arms; and the gratitude of my heart will ever be yours. Amen.

Bernard J. Marblo, Vero Beach, Florida,
a friend of Maryknoll

"Many saints knew little of theology. Few knew anything of psychology, but they knew how to pray and how to attain the perfect life."

✦ *Bishop James A. Walsh, M.M.,*
co-founder of the Maryknoll Society

A Prayer to St. Jude

Most holy apostle, St. Jude, faithful servant and friend of Jesus, the church honors and invokes you universally, as the patron of hopeless cases, of things almost despaired of. Pray for me, I am so helpless and alone. Make use, I implore you, of that particular privilege given to you, to bring visible and speedy help where help is almost despaired of.

Come to my assistance in this great need that I may receive the consolation and help of heaven in all my necessities, tribulations, and sufferings, particularly *(your request)* and that I may praise God with you and all the elect forever. I promise, O blessed St. Jude, to be ever mindful of this great favor, to always honor you as my special and powerful patron, and to gratefully encourage devotion to you. Amen.

Madalen Sugrue, Anaconda, Montana,
a friend of Maryknoll, traditional prayer

A Prayer to St. Thérèse
(My Novena Rose Prayer)

O little Thérèse of the Child Jesus, please pick for me a rose from the heavenly gardens and send it to me as a message of love.

O little Flower of Jesus, ask God today to grant the favors I now place with confidence in your hands *(mention specific requests . . .)*.

St. Thérèse, help me to always believe as you did, in God's great love for me so that I might imitate your "little way" each day. Amen.

Mary Mahoney, Dayton, Ohio,
a friend of Maryknoll

Trust

Surely God is my salvation;
I will trust, and will not be afraid,
for the LORD GOD is my strength and my might.
ISAIAH 12:2

We have our hope set on the living God, who is the
Savior of all people, especially of those who believe.
1 TIMOTHY 4:10

How wonderful to have a best friend to confide in, someone we trust with all our heart. To whom we can tell anything, and admit everything, even our darkest sins. Someone kind, loving, wise, and there for us morning, noon, and night. Someone who loves us no matter what, who smiles upon our darkness and sees only light.

Wouldn't it be wonderful to have someone like that with us right now? Let us pray.

❧

Father,
I abandon myself into your hands;
do with me what you will.
Whatever you may do, I thank you;
I am ready for all, I accept all.

Let only your will be done in me,
and in all your creatures.
I wish no more than this, O Lord.

Into your hands I commend my soul;
I offer it to you
with all the love of my heart,
for I love you, Lord,
and so need to give myself,
to surrender myself into your hands,
without reserve,
and with boundless confidence,
for you are my Father.

Father Fidelis Goodman, M.M.,
Maryknoll, New York

Larry Schierhoff, Sr., Kansas City, Missouri,
a friend of Maryknoll, a favorite prayer
of his brother, Bishop Andy Schierhoff,
the Pando, Bolivia, adapted
from a prayer of Charles de Foucauld

Your will, Lord,
only your will.

Marilyn Nowlin, San Antonio, Texas,
a friend of Maryknoll

Father, you gave us your best gift, Jesus Christ your Son, our Lord, to be our savior, brother, and strength in food and drink and word. Let us trust in you and in one another and imitate Jesus' wholehearted giving of himself. Accept our gifts, accept us, all of us, and transform us into your body, the church in the world. Amen.

Megan McKenna,
from Mary, Mother of All Nations
(Orbis Books, 2000)

Knowing you as my friend, I simply say,
    Jesus, I love you.
When I am tired, I'll still try to say,
    Jesus, I love you.
When I find it hard to forgive, I'll remember to say,
    Jesus, I love you.
When darkness comes and I don't know where you are,
I'll find you by saying,
    Jesus, I love you.
What trouble can shake me, what suffering can overcome
        me
if I always repeat,
    Jesus, I love you.
For the joys you give me, for the graces you grant me,
    my thanks will always be,
    Jesus, I love you.
And when the evening of life comes and you invite me home,
let me say one last time here below,
    Jesus, I love you.

Cathi Ward, Toledo, Ohio, a friend of Maryknoll, a
prayer of Father Thomas Garrity, M.M.,
from Maryknoll *magazine*

God Alone

No one worth serving but God:
No one so tender, so grateful.
No one worth trusting but God:
No friend so unchanging, so faithful.
No one worth loving but God:
No heart holds his wealth of affection.
No one worth seeking but God—
In His exquisite, endless perfection.

Phyllis A. Waldsmith, Edina, Minnesota,
a friend of Maryknoll,
a prayer of Kathleen Donegan from a
prayer book published in 1926 in Ireland

I know nothing about you, yet I dare to mention you—
Who are you, you whom I call upon, you in whom I trust?
And who am I to try to express you?
You are rich in goodness and mercy and you know every-
      thing.
You are the peace without which no being can exist.
You watch over all things and your infinite compassion
      gathers us together,
O Mighty One!
You are also and above all the Hidden One,
who wants to reveal himself in the depth of my heart;
beyond names and forms, beyond myself,
you ask me to come to the desert
where my song one day will cease at the shores of darkness
and in secret I will hear that there is no God but God.

Father Doug Venne, M.M., Dhaka, Bangladesh,
from a Muslim prayer hanging on a wall
in Diang, Chittagong, Bangladesh

Lord Jesus, I pray that you never deny me your light, which I need so much so that I can find the way of salvation. Lord, you are the hope of the whole world. Lord, accompany me so that I may feel in my innermost heart that love, faith, peace, life and hope of salvation.

Sister Joan Uhlen, M.M.,
Chacraseca, Nicaragua,
a prayer of Cruz Clarisa Hernandez
(translated by Sister Bernice Kita, M.M.)

I cannot change the world, Lord, no matter how I try.
Only You have power of things beneath the sky,
But still You do encourage the little things I do,
Like showing love and kindness and telling folks of You.
I cannot change the world, Lord, but I can love and care.
I know that You will nurture each seed I plant out there.
And you will bring forth blossoms from little things I do.
I cannot change the world, Lord, but I'll do my best for
    you.

Connie Lubrano, Brooklyn, New York,
a friend of Maryknoll

I tell you, solemnly, whatever you ask for in prayer, believe that you have received it, and it will be yours, says the Lord. (Mark 11:23–24)
    ❧ *Marianne K. Lowe and Janice M. Lowe,*
    Parma, Ohio, friends of Maryknoll,
    from the Communion Antiphon
    for the 33rd Sunday in Ordinary Time

O God, accept us
and do not throw us away.
O God, place us in your navel
and do not take us out again.
O God, place us in the flame of your womb
and do not take us out of it.
O God, place us in the folds of your black garment
and do not take us out of them.
O God, place us in the whiteness of your womb
and do not take us out again.
O God, place us under your wings
and do not put us down again.
O God, carry us under your sweet armpits
And do not put us down again.
O God, carry us on your back
and do not put us down again.

*Sister Janice McLaughlin, M.M.,
Harare, Zimbabwe, a Maasai song translated
by Jan Voshaar, MHM, from A Warm, Moist, Salty
God: Women Journeying towards Wisdom
by Edwina Gateley (Source Books, 1993)*

Have no anxiety at all, but in everything, by prayer and petition, with thanksgiving, make your requests known to God. Then the peace of God that surpasses all understanding will guard your hearts and minds in Christ Jesus. (Philippians 4:6–7)
❧ *Mrs. Raul Tuban, Gaithersburg, Maryland,
a friend of Maryknoll*

Dear Lord, when I am crushed and weary, when the hope I have lived for has gone, when sorrows and trials that I dare not reveal to any make my soul sink almost unto death, when I look in vain for someone to understand me, one who will enter into my miseries, make me then remember that there is Someone who knows every fiber of my heart, every sorrow, every pain special to my peculiar nature, and who deeply sympathizes with me.

Compassionate Jesus! When shared with You, the cross becomes lighter and in your heart I find rest and strength.

Lucy Kinn, Hankinson, North Dakota,
a friend of Maryknoll,
from the Catholic Devotional Prayer Book

Lord, you are ever attentive even to the most humble prayer. Your divine providence ever watches over us. It directs the flight of the bird and lets fall the dew to refresh the flower of the field, providing with tender solicitude for the needs of all creation.

I believe, Lord, that you will hear me and I hope in you. In moments of sadness and discouragement, I will place all my confidence in you alone. Give me, Lord, that courage which will help me to serve you to the end and will enkindle my faith in your all-loving care. Grant that humbly, confidently, and with a child's simplicity I may ever trust in your powerful and never failing providence. Amen.

Connie Spadell, Lattimer Mines, Pennsylvania,
a friend of Maryknoll

Hope

We still hope, remembering
The voice of the dove in our land.
Announcing once again that
Even in bitter moments, we were
Never alone. We still hope, that
We will rise up and out to the
Fields. To see if the plants are
Flowering. If the joy has
Returned. If the corn is ripe.
And there You will show us Your
Love. And we will show You ours.

A prayer from Mexico

Suscipe

My God, I am Yours for time and eternity. Teach me to cast myself entirely into the arms of Your loving Providence with the most lively, unlimited confidence in Your compassionate, tender pity. Grant me, O most merciful Redeemer, that whatever You ordain or permit may be acceptable to me.

Take from my heart all painful anxiety; suffer nothing to sadden me but sin, nothing to delight me but the hope of coming to the possession of You, my God and my all, in Your everlasting Kingdom. Amen.

Jeanne W. Bone, Menlo Park, California,
a friend of Maryknoll,
a prayer of Catherine McAuley,
foundress of the Sisters of Mercy

Do not look forward to what may happen tomorrow. The same everlasting Father who cares for you today will take care of you tomorrow and every day. Either He will shield you from suffering or He will give you unfailing strength to bear it.

Be at peace then, put aside all anxious thoughts and imaginations, and say continually:

The Lord is my strength and my shield; my heart has trusted in Him and I am helped. He is not only with me but in me and I in Him.

Betty Cafiero, Monroe Township, New Jersey,
a friend of Maryknoll,
a prayer of St. Francis de Sales (1181–1226)

Dear Lord, help me to remember that nothing is going to happen to me today that You and I can't handle together. Amen.

Jo Sullivan Coyle, Tempe, Arizona,
a friend of Maryknoll, author unknown

I know that when the stress has grown too strong,
    Thou wilt be there;
that when the waiting seems so long,
    Thou hearest prayer.
that through the crash of falling worlds,
    Thou holdest me,
that life and death and all are Thine eternally.

The Carmelite Monastery,
Flemington, New Jersey,
a prayer of Janet Erskine Stuart, R.S.C.J.

Solitude

Heavenly Comforter,
Now that I am alone,
Let me not feel lonely.
Open my heart to your peace,
That I might find harmony within myself.
Teach me to use these
Solitary moments to draw
Closer to thee.

Enrich my soul with your love
In this blessed quiet.

A Maryknoll Missioner

For everything that has been,
  Thanks!
For all that is to come,
  Yes!

*Dona Gallagher, Gatesville, Texas,
a friend of Maryknoll,
a prayer by Dag Hammarskjöld*

Lord, on this beautiful morning, when you have given
me strength to come to be with you and my baptized brothers and sisters, by the grace of the Father and the Son and
the Holy Spirit, Lord, give me the strength to remain firm
in our faith. Like the church of Christ, I await your return. Help me, your faithful servant, do this.

*Sister Joan Uhlen, M.M.,
Chacraseca, Nicaragua,
a prayer of Antonio S.R.
(translated by Sister Bernice Kita, M.M.)*

Footprints

One night a man had a dream. He dreamed he was walking along the beach with the Lord. Across the sky flashed scenes from his life. For each scene, he noticed two sets of footprints in the sand: one belonging to him, and the other to the Lord.

When the last scene of his life flashed before him, he looked back at the footprints in the sand. He noticed that many times along the path of his life there was only one set of footprints. He also noticed that it happened at the lowest and saddest times of his life. This really bothered him and he questioned the Lord about it.

"Lord, you said that once I decided to follow you, you'd walk with me all the way. But I have noticed that during the most troublesome times in my life, there is only one set of footprints. I don't understand why when I needed you most you would leave me." The Lord replied, "My son, my precious child, I love you and I would never leave you. During your times of trial and suffering, when you see only one set of footprints, it was then that I carried you."

❧ *Robert A. Hyland,*
North Falmouth, Massachusetts,
a friend of Maryknoll,
author unknown

Forgiveness

"Do not judge, and you will not be judged; do not condemn, and you will not be condemned. Forgive, and you will be forgiven."

LUKE 6:37

Peter came and said to him, "Lord, if my brother sins against me, how often should I forgive? As many as seven times?" Jesus said to him, "Not seven times, but, I tell you, seventy-seven times."

MATTHEW 18:21–22

"The best way to define forgiveness," wrote psychiatrist Thomas Hora, "is to give up blaming." What a helpful spiritual definition that is also!

To forgive is to imitate God. God is love, and love never blames. Love forgives. Seventy times seven times, which means all the time. What an awesome, wonderful gift forgiveness is! And who wouldn't like to experience it, right now? Let us pray.

❧

Out of the depths I cry to you, Lord
  Lord hear my voice
  be attentive to my cry

If you remember our sin
  who could bear it?
No, your glory is your forgiveness

My soul hopes in the Lord
  I take my stand on his word
More than the sleepless awaiting the dawn
  my soul awaits him

As a vigiler awaits the dawn
  let his friends await the Lord

For with him is grace in abundance!
  Out of the depths
  I take my stand on his word.

Daniel Berrigan, from Uncommon Prayer,
based on Psalm 130 (Orbis Books, 1998)

Eternal Father, as we pass through this life,
help us to remember to love, forgive, and forget.
We know that you are with us at all times,
just waiting for us to come to you.
May we find in you and others peace and forgiveness.
Most Holy Spirit, come down upon us
and guide us to do your holy will.
Eternal Father, may your blessing come down upon us
     and remain forever.

*Joe Lombardo, Greenwood, Indiana,
a long-time friend and supporter of Maryknoll*

O My God, Pardon Me

O my God, pardon me, pardon me for my coldness, my cowardliness, my wasted time, my pride, my love of my own will, forgive me my weakness and unfaithfulness, the confusion of my thoughts, my forgetfulness of your presence. Forgive, forgive my sins, all the faults of my life. . . . I thank you for your many graces.

My Lord and my God, come to my aid, help me on whom you have showered your gifts so that I might be converted, and let me use the gifts that you still offer me so that I may do whatever you ask of me, whatever, in your infinite goodness, you call me to do, I who am so unworthy.

Turn my heart toward you, my God, for the sake of our Lord Jesus Christ. . . . You are all-powerful over your creatures, you can do all things in me. Give me a right mind, give me the wisdom that you promise to all who ask for it. Convert my heart and let me glorify you to the utmost till my last breath and through all eternity. I ask this in the name of our Savior Jesus Christ. Amen. Amen. Amen.

Charles de Foucauld, North Africa,
from Charles de Foucauld
(Orbis Books, 1999)

O Lord, who has mercy on all, take away from me my sins and mercifully kindle in me the fire of your Holy Spirit. Take away from me the heart of stone and give me a heart of flesh, a heart to love and adore you, a heart to delight in you, to follow and to enjoy you, for Christ's sake.

St. Ambrose (339–397)

Lord, teach us to forgive:
to look deep into the hearts
of those who wound us,
so that we may glimpse,
in that dark, still water,
not just the reflection
of our own face
but yours as well.

*Sheila Cassidy, England,
from* Good Friday People
(Orbis Books, 1995)

Forgiveness

Gentle Jesus,
I have been wronged
And betrayed. My being is filled
With hurt and fury. I want to
Lash out and strike down my
Enemy in retribution.

Please help me abide by Your
Teaching, to turn the other cheek.
Give me the strength to combat
Wickedness with love, to forgive
Those who would see me harmed.

In this and all things, help me to
Follow Your divine example.

*Jackie Ring,
from an old Maryknoll prayer booklet*

Who Am I to Judge?

I have not heard the music within your being nor felt the rhythm of your life. . . . How can I criticize your song or even your singing?

I have not dreamed your dreams nor seen your visions nor designed your castles. . . . How can I say you are walking in the wrong direction?

I have not plumbed the depths of your feelings nor felt the intensity of your needs nor known the agony of your hurts. . . . How can I say you should not cry?

I have not known the questions you have asked nor heard the answers you were given nor witnessed your encounter with mystery. . . . How can I say you are not living?

I have not walked the path of your youth nor stood at the crossroads of your decisions nor journeyed the roads of your daily living. . . . How can I say your life is not true?

I have not known the pain of your sufferings nor the intensity of your battles nor the humiliations of your defeats. . . . How can I say you do not try?

Yet, my sister, my brother, these I have both said and done. Forgive me.

Kathleen Stephens, San Antonio, Texas,
a friend of Maryknoll,
a prayer by Monsignor Bernard Powers

"Forgiveness is the fragrance the violet sheds on the heel that has crushed it."

⤚ *Mark Twain*

Blessings

---

*May the God of peace sanctify you entirely; and may
your spirit and soul and body be kept sound and
blameless at the coming of our Lord Jesus Christ.*

1 THESSALONIANS 5:23

*Grow in the grace and knowledge of our Lord and
Savior Jesus Christ. To him be the glory both now and
to the day of eternity. Amen.*

2 PETER 3:18

As we strive to follow the footsteps of Jesus and grow in closeness to God, our lives lived each day can become blessings. While most of us will never achieve the holiness of the saints, our caring for others through our prayers and actions will bless their lives and ours into eternity. Let us pray.

❧

May God bless you with discomfort at easy answers, half-truths, and superficial relationships, so that you will live deep in your heart.

May God bless you with anger at injustice, oppression, and exploitation of people and the earth so that you will work for justice, equity, and peace.

May God bless you with tears to shed for those who suffer so you will reach out your hands to comfort them and change their pain into joy.

And may God bless you with the foolishness to think that you can make a difference in the world, so you will do the things which others say cannot be done.

Ellie Hays, Maryknoll Affiliate,
Sparks, Nevada

A Father's Blessing

Child of mine,
mystery wrapped
GIFT.
the world like you
is new all the time.
PAIN
grows there.
Hold it to yourself
and teach it
to dance!
JOY

Joe Mortell, Joliet, Illinois,
a friend of Maryknoll,
a prayer by Sister Jean Pruitt, M.M.

Strengthened by the Spirit of God and by the love of your sisters and brothers, go forth with confidence and courage to live the good news! May you trust and dare enough to:

Believe God's love so deeply that you will watch for and celebrate signs of God's power in you and in all others.

Trust your ability to know what is "enough" and to struggle in solidarity with those who are poor.

Live gently, letting your heart's desires lead you, letting God be at work and at rest in you.

Celebrate and live Eucharist enough to cherish the earth and all creation, to trust our identity as a multicultural community, and to form inclusive communities, following Jesus' example of eating with the excluded.

Let your whole being rejoice in God who has done great things for us.

Sister Barbara Paleczny, SSND,
San Antonio, Texas

Vocation Blessing

I hope you come to find that which gives life a deep meaning for you. Something worth living for—maybe even worth dying for—something that energizes you, enthuses you, enables you to keep moving ahead. I can't tell you what it might be—that's for you to find, to choose, to love. I can just encourage you to start looking, and support you in the search.

Mary Zoppi, Heathcote, Australia,
a friend of Maryknoll, from a letter that
Maryknoll Sister Ita Ford wrote to her niece
shortly before Sister Ita was martyred
in El Salvador on December 2, 1980

In blessing our foreheads,
we claim the power of reason,
to know that path that leads to the fulfillment
of our hopes for a liberated humankind.

In blessing our eyes,
we claim the power of vision,
to see clearly the forces of life and death in our midst.

In blessing our ears,
we claim the power to hear the Spirit of God
as She speaks to us within.

In blessing our lips,
we claim the power to speak the truth about our experi-
        ence;
we claim power to name ourselves and our God.

In blessing our hands,
we claim our powers as creators of a new humanity
liberated from fear, ignorance, and oppression.

In blessing our feet,
we claim the power to walk the paths of our courageous
        forebears and to forge new paths where they are
        needed.

In blessing each other,
we claim the creative power that rests collectively
in our shared struggle as women and men.
We choose to extend this power in service to a world in
        need.

May our lives be blessings to each other.
Amen.

Maryknoll Mission Association of the Faithful

Blessing of Mothers

God, our Father, we ask you to bless all the mothers here present today, together with those others who, in various ways, fulfill a mother's role. Give them your love, that they may love those entrusted to them with the love which only they as mothers can give.

Give them your strength, that they may never weary of the demanding role that is theirs, always ready to support, advise, encourage and sustain those who are so precious to them. Give them your warmth, that they may radiate to their children the human and divine qualities of compassion, understanding, patience, and kindness.

Above all, give them your joy and peace, that they may always know the special place they have in your heart—that you love them as you gave your love to Mary, the mother of Jesus, your son. On this Mothers' Day, may these special people who give so much to others, so unselfishly and generously, know that you are with them always.

Joseph A. Hynes, Freehold, New Jersey,
a friend of Maryknoll

Let nothing trouble thee,
Let nothing frighten thee,
All things pass away;
God never changes,
Patience obtains all things.
Nothing is wanting to him who possesses God.
God alone suffices.

The Carmelite Monastery,
Flemington, New Jersey,
St. Teresa's bookmark

A Blessing Prayer for Teachers, Preachers, and All Who Evangelize

Blessed are you Lord God of all creation,
for in your faithful and generous love
you have always cared to bless us with wise and holy
teachers and preachers,
men and women from whom we have drawn
inspiration, guidance, and courage.

We give you thanks for their imagination,
for through their stories of our lives
we have grown to be more hopeful.
Amen.

We praise you for their openness to your Word,
for through their obedience
we have learned to be less fearful of our own conversions.
Amen.

We rejoice in their willingness to leave behind
so many of the securities and satisfactions of our world,
for through their unselfish love
we have become more convinced that God can be trusted
            with our lives too.
Amen.

Holy Spirit of God,
fill your servant *(name)*
with a deep, rich sureness of his/her goodness and
            purpose
in your plan for our world.
Convince *(him/her)* now and forever
that within the company of your friends
there are no little people and no little places,

but only ones where your gracefulness is found,
and your life born among us.

May each of us—and all who know *(him/her)*—
now more surely and easily
bear the love of God—Father, Son, and Spirit—to one
    another. Amen.

Father Michael Henning, Pastor,
All Saints Parish, Saint Peters, Missouri,
a friend of Maryknoll

A Blessing for Priests

May you be steadfast on your journey, powered by the
message of love and the command to serve.

May you wear the Gospel on your sleeve so that all who
know you may understand the value of justice, the need
for kindness, the grace of forgiveness.

As you break bread with all who approach the table,
may you be blessed with a song of freedom and a prayer of
hope, so that all may come to know deep peace and hear
the good news that Jesus is risen and present among us.

Father Dennis Cleary, M.M., Maryknoll, New York,
a prayer by Sister Margaret Cessna, H.M.

"May you be in heaven half an hour
before the devil knows you're dead!"

❧ *Barbara Hussey Riggins,*
Walnut Creek, California,
a friend of Maryknoll

Beatitudes for Women

Happy is she who suffers with the very young,
the very old, and the very lonely,
for she has compassion.

Happy is she who greets the world with joy,
laughter and anticipation,
for she has courage.

Happy is she who lives not where she chooses,
but where she is sent,
for she has freedom.

Happy is she who speaks gently, lives humbly,
for she has dignity.

Happy is she who listens and hears and extends her hands,
for she has understanding.

Happy is she who lives simply, loves deeply,
for she has sincerity.

Happy is she who lives intensively, and sings life's alleluia,
for she has awareness.

Happy is she who has compassion and courage,
freedom and dignity, understanding,
sincerity and awareness.
For she is woman.

Sister Elizabeth Lee, M.M.,
Gallup, New Mexico

Table Graces

Whether we eat or drink, or whatsoever we do, let us do all to the glory of God. *(1 Corinthians 10:31)*

⁖

God, grant that in partaking of this food, we may be mindful of those who go hungry. Strengthen our purpose so that by our daily deeds of service the day may be brought nearer when no one shall want for food or fellowship.

⁖

Noisy, vain repetitions are an abomination unto thee, O God. Make us to pray our prayer with loving heart and hidden words, for thou will do all that is necessary for our daily needs. *(Egyptian, c. 900 B.C.E.)*

⁖

God bless the providers, the dividers, and the devourers.

⁖

O God, we have very much [refrigerators and cars and telephones] and our world of things is very great. Help us not to confuse things with people, because thou has taught us to use things and to love people and not the other way around. Amen. *(Richard Wong, Hawaii)*

⁖

For good food and good company, we praise thee, Lord. Sustain also, we beseech thee, the needs of others, so that we may always give thee thanks, through Jesus Christ our Lord. Amen. *(From the Latin)*

For the farmers who have worked that we may eat,
For those who have bought and sold this food,
For those who have prepared it,
And most of all, for you, who planned it,
We thank you, Lord.

✑

Praised be my Lord for our mother the earth,
which sustains us and keeps us, and brings forth
fruits, and flowers of many colors, and grass.
Praised be my Lord for all those who pardon one
another for his love's sake, and who endure
weakness and tribulation. . . . Praise ye and bless
ye the Lord, and give thanks unto him, and serve
him with great humility. *(St. Francis of Assisi)*

✑

Father, for our daily food, for the light of thy
truth, for thy hearing of our prayers, and for every
manifestation of thy presence, we thank and praise
thee. Amen. *(From the Chinese)*

✑

Ask for what you want, thank God for what
you receive, and don't grumble.

✑

Thou has given so much to us, give us one
thing more: a grateful heart.

*✑ These graces before meals appeared
in* The Maryknoll International Cookbook,
*compiled by Sister Mary Carol Cannon
and Sister Mary Corde Lorang
(Orbis Books, 1973).*

God be in my head, and in my understanding;
God be in my eyes, and in my looking;
God be in my mouth, and in my speaking;
God be in my heart, and in my thinking;
God be at my end, and at my departing.

Helen T. Michalka, Fairfield, Connecticut,
a friend of Maryknoll,
a prayer from the Sarum Primer
(sixteenth century)

Dear Jesus, bless each person who has touched my life in the past, the present, and in the future, whether they are living or deceased.

Martha Mary Keen, Oak Park, Illinois,
a friend of Maryknoll

An Irish Blessing

Christ as a light, illumine and guide me.
Christ as a shield, o'ershadow and cover me.
Christ be before me, behind me, about me.
Christ this day be within and without me.
Christ, the lowly and meek, be in the heart of those to
      whom I speak,
In the mouth of each who speaks to me,
In all who draw near me, or see me, or hear me. Amen.

Annamarie Cook, Chicago, Illinois,
a friend of Maryknoll,
from St. Patrick's Breastplate

A New Irish Blessing

May there be springs enough in your life
to outlast the winters.

May there be guitars (and drums) enough
to lift your spirits whenever you need it.

May you be gentle enough
to comfort those who are hurting,
But revolutionary enough
to bring heaven to those who need it now.

May there always be a leprechaun near you
to bring out laughter and dance
and the child in you.

And may God always have room enough
for you in the palm of her hand.

Tom Gilsenan, Iowa City, Iowa,
a friend of Maryknoll

Invocation

May all blessings come to me,
May all gods protect me,
By the grace of the Sacred Teachings,
May weal ever abound in me!

Father Jim Kofski, M.M., Bangkok, Thailand,
from a Buddhist prayer from
Professor Kirti Bunchua, dean of the
School of Philosophy and Religious Studies
at Assumption University in Bangkok

Africa, bless the Lord
All you tribes and districts, bless the Lord
From Dar es Salaam to Kampala, bless the Lord
From Mombasa to Lusaka, bless the Lord
Here let all the works of the Lord bless the Lord
Praise and bless him forever.

All you BIG things, bless the Lord
Mt. Kilimanjaro and Lake Victoria
The Rift Valley and the Serengeti Plain
Elephants and African chiefs and endless plains
All you big things, bless the Lord
Praise and bless him forever.

All you TINY things, bless the Lord
Busy insects and drops of rain
Tiny colorful birds and small gazelles
Our simple lifestyle, our newborn economy
Our infant children and our new faith
All you tiny things, bless the Lord
Praise and bless him forever.

All you SHARP things, bless the Lord
Sisal plant tips and tall lake reeds
Maasai spears and Kikuyu hunting arrows
Our gifted young people
Our promising African priests and religious and catechists
All you sharp things, bless the Lord
Praise and bless him forever.

All you SOFT things, bless the Lord
Cotton and ashes and feathers and sand
A town by the lake, a straw-roofed hut
African children with their gentleness and joy

All you soft things, bless the Lord
Praise and bless him forever.

All you SWEET things, bless the Lord
Wild honey and mangos and sugar cane
Oranges and bananas and corn roasted over a fire
Clean water and abundant harvest and good health
Kindness and love and joy and peace
All you sweet things, bless the Lord
Praise and bless him forever.

All you BITTER things—even you, bless the Lord
Maize beer and sour milk and quinine and blue soap
Long hours at plowing and weeding and threshing
The pain that comes with no medicine and no money
The anguish from having so little to give our children
All you bitter things—even you, bless the Lord
Praise and bless him forever.

All you SWIFT things, bless the Lord
A wild pig, a fleeing snake, herds of migrating animals
The endless running and activity of countless children
A lion ready to spring, girls pounding corn
Swift moving trucks stopped by rivers more swift
All you swift things, bless the Lord
Praise and bless him forever.

All you SLOW things, bless the Lord
Curious giraffe and thin cows searching for grass
The peaceful countryside and the slow pace of life
Spending all day making mud bricks to build a home
Sitting by the roadside with nowhere to go
All you slow things, bless the Lord
Praise and bless him forever.

All you LOUD things, bless the Lord
Charging buffalo and midnight hyenas
A sudden downpour on a metal church roof
Feast-day drums and shouting school children and church
      choirs
All you loud things, bless the Lord
Praise and bless him forever.

Finally, all you QUIET things, bless the Lord
Quiet trees and quiet visits and quiet meals
A small church bell ringing in a big countryside
Maasai children playing, a mother with her baby
All you quiet things, bless the Lord
Praise and bless him forever.

Joanne Miya, MMAF, Tanzania,
from a prayer composed by students
of Morogoro High School, Tanzania, 1963,
under the direction of
Sister Josephine Lucker, M.M.

African Prayers of Blessing, Sending Forth, and Healing

The person officiating is instructed to sprinkle water or another
substance such as flour or incense in the four directions of the
universe while saying:

Facing east: For our ancestors of the distant past.
Facing west: For our recent living dead.
Facing north: For our living.
Facing south: For our yet unborn.

Father Joseph Healey, M.M.,
Dar es Salaam, Tanzania

May God go with you!
May you go with God!
May your path be free of danger!
May you escape all mishaps!
My God bear you in peace!
May you meet with kindness!
May God take care of you!
May God walk with you!
May God be with those left behind!
May you pass the night with God!
May you remain with God!

Various African Blessings

A Christmas Prayer

Please bless us, dearest Lord,
On this your special day.
Bless the family gathered here
As we bow our heads to pray.

We thank you for your blessings
showered from above;
We thank you for the gifts bestowed,
And for a family's love.

Now let us hold each other's hands
And say a little prayer
That God will bless the absent ones,
And families everywhere. Amen.

Sylvia Scannell,
Brick, New Jersey,
a friend of Maryknoll

A Prayer for after Mass

May this blessing, which I receive from your hands, be an anticipation of the one I shall receive on the day of my death, when I shall be called up to appear before thy divine tribunal to give an account of my life. On that day, dear Lord, have mercy on me, forgive me my sins, and bring me to life everlasting. Amen.

Nell W. Crawford (94 years of age),
Lower Burrell, Pennsylvania,
a friend of Maryknoll

Hymn of Universal Love

Let him cultivate a mind of boundless love
For all, throughout the universe,
In all its height, depth and breadth,
Love that is unrestricted,
And beyond hatred or enmity.

Whether he stands, walks, sits or lies down,
As long as he is awake,
Let him maintain this "love-awareness"
Deemed here a Divine State.

Holding no wrong view, virtuous,
And with vision of the Ultimate,
Having overcome all sensual desire,
Never in a womb is he born again.

Father Jim Kofski, M.M.,
Bangkok, Thailand,
from a Buddhist prayer

I Said a Prayer for You Today

I said a prayer for you today
And know God must have heard.
I felt the answer in my heart
Although He spoke no word.

I didn't ask for wealth or fame
(I knew you wouldn't mind)—
I asked Him to send treasures
Of a far more lasting kind.
I asked that He'd be near you
At the start of each new day
To grant you health and blessings
And friends to share your way.
I asked for happiness for you
In all things great and small—
but it was for His loving care
I prayed the most of all.

❧ *Mrs. Wilfred J. Deutsch, San Jacinto, California,*
a friend of Maryknoll, author unknown

A Traditional Irish Blessing

May the road rise to meet you.
May the wind be always at your back.
May the sun shine upon your face.
The rains fall soft upon your fields
And, until we meet again,
May God hold you in the palm of his hand.

Barbara Hussey Riggins,
Walnut Creek, California,
a friend of Maryknoll

Praise and Thanksgiving

O give thanks unto the LORD; for he is good:
for his mercy endureth for ever.

PSALM 136:1

Be thankful . . . and with gratitude in your hearts sing
psalms, hymns, and spiritual songs to God. And whatever
you do, in word or deed, do everything in the name of the
Lord Jesus, giving thanks to God the Father through him.

COLOSSIANS 3:15–17

A grateful heart pumps joy into our life, and into the lives of everyone around us. There is no higher prayer than praise, and no higher praise than gratitude.

We have so much to be grateful for:

God is with us.
We are members of the family of God.
We have eyes to see what is good, beautiful, and true.
God guides us, and hears our prayers.
God loves and blesses and forgives us all the time.
We can love and bless and forgive our brothers and
    sisters in Christ.
We can trust God, all the time. He is our salvation.

Let us pray. And pray again. Thank you, God!

❧

— PRAYERS OF PRAISE —

We praise You, God of all the earth,
and all Your ways we bless.
In You all love begins and ends.
Your universal love transcends
our own dividedness.

We call to You with words we clothe
in cultures of our own.
You rise above all cultic claims
to answer to our many names,
a God as yet unknown.

O Wisdom, wait within us,
wake our weary hearts to praise,
empowering the powerless
and strengthening with gentleness,
till all embrace Your ways.

Our many paths all lead to You
in every time and place.
Our hearts rejoice in serving You,
make all we are and all we do
a channel of Your grace.

We run to You, O Sacred Source
of hope and harmony.
Our work on earth will not be done,
till human hearts all beat as one
in global unity.

*Miriam Therese Winter, India,
from* The Singer and the Song
(Orbis Books, 1999)

O Lord in whom all things live,
who commanded us to seek you,
who are always ready to be found:
to know you is life,
to serve you is freedom,
to praise you is our souls' delight.
We bless you and adore you,
we worship you and magnify you,
we give thanks to you for your great glory,
through Jesus Christ our Lord.

St. Augustine (354–430)

God Gives Us Power

God has given us the power

To create beauty
To make another smile
To be a healing presence in someone's sorrow
To bring justice to the oppressed
To console those in difficulty
To bring peace and joy to others
To help those in need
To laugh and enjoy life
To do good and turn from evil
To forgive those who have hurt us
And, most of all, to love.

Let us pray that God will continue to grace us with his
love and mercy
And to spread that love to others during our journey.

*Iris Perez, Orbis Books,
Maryknoll, New York*

Praise Be to You for Life

Praise be to you, O Lord, for life
    and for my intense desire to live;
praise be to you for the mystery of love
    and for my intense desire to be a lover;
praise be to you for this day
    and another chance to live and love.

Thank you, Lord,
    for friends who stake their claim in my heart,
    for enemies who disturb my soul and bump my ego,
    for tuba players,
        and story tellers,
            and trapeze troupes.

Thank you, Lord,
    for singers of songs,
    for teachers of songs,
        who help me sing along the way,
    . . . and for listeners.

Thank you, Lord,
    for those who attempt beauty
        rather than curse ugliness,
    for those who take stands
        rather than take polls,
    for those who risk being right
        rather than pandering to be liked,
    for those who do something
        rather than talking about everything.

Lord, grant me grace, then,
and a portion of your spirit
that I may so live

as to give others cause
>to be thankful for me;
thankful because I have not forgotten
>how to hope,
>>how to laugh,
>>>how to say "I'm sorry,"
>how to forgive,
>>how to bind up wounds,
>>>how to dream,
>how to cry,
>>how to pray,
>how to love when it is hard,
>>and how to dare when it is dangerous.
Un-dam me, Lord,
that praise may flow more easily from me
>than wants,
thanks more readily
>than complaints.
Praise be to you, Lord, for life;
Praise be to you for another chance to live.

Angela Kochera, Rocky River, Ohio,
a friend of Maryknoll,
from Guerrillas of Grace *by Ted Loder, ©1984*
Innisfree Press. Reprinted with permission.

You are beauty, you are gentleness.
You are our protector, our guardian and defender.
You are courage, you are our haven and our hope.
You are our faith, our great consolation.
You are our eternal life, great and wonderful Lord,
God almighty, merciful Savior.

St. Francis of Assisi (1181–1226)

The Martyr's Prayer

O Heavenly Father, praise be to you who have given life to all peoples through the passion of your Son and the power of your Holy Spirit. Through your miraculous providence, our ancestors themselves discovered the faith and in persecution and many trials courageously witnessed to the Truth and brightened this land with the light of salvation.

O Lord, we thank you for your great graces, and we pray that this land may be renewed with the flame of the Holy Spirit. We pray that following the example of our martyred saints, we may live deeply in the mystery of Christ's death and resurrection and become one in faith and love. Joyfully proclaiming the Gospel, we beseech you that the grace of salvation may spring up and enlighten even the darkness of the north.

O Lord, help us offer our whole being to bring the Truth to this age, and with fraternal love and the evangelical spirit of poverty, to become a church in solidarity with the poor and powerless. Grant also that our martyrs bring your light to all people. Finally, make present the kingdom of the Father to the whole world. We make this prayer in the name of Jesus the Lord. Amen.

Father Gerard Hammond, M.M.,
Seoul, Korea,
from a favorite Korean prayer

A Jamaican Chorus

He is here, alleluia!
He is here, amen!
He is here, holy, holy!
I will bless his name again.
He is here, listen closely,
He is calling out your name.
He is here, you can touch him,
You will never be the same.

Marie Iadavaia,
Bronxville, New York,
a friend of Maryknoll,
from Company *(Spring 1999)*

Gentle Father who sent us Jesus
To show us the human face of love,
We praise you.

As we enter this new millennium
We ask you to dry the tears of our sorrows
And give us the courage to make this
Covenant with you:

We promise to start anew.
We will mirror your love,
We will care for your universe,
We will forgive others as you forgive us.

Bertha Perron,
Vergennes, Vermont,
from a prayer card
of The Pallottines

O Holy Spirit

O Holy Spirit,
Mighty defender,
To all who love you,
Comfort you give.
Ev'rywhere present,
Fountain of virtues,
Without your kindness,
No one could live.

O Holy Spirit,
Treasury of blessings,
Come, as was promised,
Life-giving flame.
Come, dwell within us,
Quicken our cool hearts,
Strengthen our purpose
To praise your name.

Eugene G. Opsasnick, Dalton, Pennsylvania,
a friend of Maryknoll, a prayer from the
Byzantine Eastern Catholic Rite

O my God!
I love thee above all things,
with my whole heart and soul,
because thou art all good and worthy of all love.
I love my neighbor as myself for love of thee.
I forgive all who have injured me,
and ask pardon of all whom I have injured. Amen.

Bishop William J. McNaughton, M.M.,
Inchon, Korea from the
Maryknoll Fathers' Prayer Book *(1963)*

Dear Lord,
each morning when I wake
each sound I hear,
each breath I take
is all because of you.

My mind is full of grateful thoughts
and honor that is due;
my senses are alive with joy,
and all because of you.

I see you in each one I meet,
and when my day is through,
the souls I've helped each day with love
is all because of you.

Margaret M. Janacek, Wood Dale, Illinois,
a friend of Maryknoll,
written by a retired nurse/therapist
as a thank you for God's graces

Praised be my Lord for our mother the earth,
which sustains us and keep us,
and brings forth fruits, and flowers of many colors, and
    grass.

Praised be my Lord for all those who pardon one another
    for his love's sake,
and who endure weakness and tribulation. . . .

Praise ye and bless ye the Lord, and give thanks unto him,
and serve him with great humility.

St. Francis of Assisi (1181–1226)

Lord, You Were Always There

Lord, you were there when all seemed lost,
And you paid the price upon the cross.

Lord, you were there, in my deepest despair,
Watching over me, with your loving care.

Lord, you were there when there was no hope,
Guiding my way, helping me cope.

Lord, you were there when my heart was crushed,
Lifting me up with your healing touch.

Lord, you were there in all happy times too,
With grateful thanks, I am praising you.

And Lord, I know you'll be there to the very end
When you welcome me home, to my Father, my Friend.
        Amen.

Dolores Kostyak,
Braddock, Pennsylvania,
a friend of Maryknoll

"If the only prayer you said in your whole life was,
'Thank you,' that would suffice."
        ❧ *Meister Eckhart*

The Prayer of the Chalice

Father, to you I raise my whole being,
a vessel emptied of self. Accept, Lord,
this my emptiness, and so fill me with
Yourself—your light, your love, your
life—that these your precious gifts
may radiate through me and over-
flow the chalice of my heart into
the hearts of all with whom I
come in contact this day,
revealing to them
the beauty of
your joy
and
wholeness
and
the
serenity
of your peace
which nothing can destroy.

Theresa L. Tenute,
Carrollton, Texas,
a friend of Maryknoll,
author unknown

Heavenly Grace

O Lord, when I look around and see your wondrous splen-
dor,
I am filled with love and wonder at your mighty power.

You created the green valleys filled with rolling, windswept
rows of wheat
Swaying like musical notes as the wind sweeps slowly across
the fields. . . .

I can hear your voice as the breeze whispers softly in my
ear—
"Come to me if you are weary and I will give you rest—for
I am the way."

As I climb your majestic mountain tops where the air is
crisp and fresh,
I inhale your presence and feel your Holy Spirit alive within
me.

I gaze upon all your beautiful wildflowers, each reaching
up for your light,
Each flower created uniquely different in your infinite
wisdom.

O Lord, you are the giver of life—the rock of my salvation.
I lift my hands high to the heavens above in praise, and
worship
In grateful thanksgiving for your everlasting presence and
love.

Barbara Ann Muscarnera,
Sumner, Washington,
a friend of Maryknoll

— **PRAYERS OF THANKSGIVING** —

We, who gather here today,
give you thanks
for opening our eyes, lives and hearts
to people of lands beyond our horizons.

During our pilgrimages
of encounter with people
in lands no longer so far afield,
some part of us has sprouted
and seeks now to grow in the beauty of the garden of our
        hearts.

We pray that you teach us
how to care for this seedling of solidarity
of hope
of healing.
We pray for good soil, rain and sunshine
So that our seedling within
may endure the test of time and seasons.

We who gather here today
give you thanks
for worldwide hearts.

Steve Hicken, MMAF,
Castro Valley, California

A Mayan Indian Prayer

Before beginning the prayer [the one below is somewhat abbreviated], fruit, corn, beans and flowers are arranged in the form of a cross on the earth. Six candles are placed during the prayer, one at each arm of the cross and two in the center.

The prayer begins. As the prayer proceeds, the people kneel at each point. Finally, a green and a blue candle are placed at the center of the cross, which represents the center of the earth and sky. God is the heart of the earth and the heart of the sky.

(At the eastern point with a red candle)

Heart of heaven, Heart of earth, we thank you for the sun. We offer you this candle that represents the blood that courses through our bodies and the heat we receive from the sun.

(At the western point with a black candle)

We give thanks for the night with which you have gifted us, with the hope of another new dawn, and for our ancestors who have died. *(A long list of names recorded in a notebook may be recited.)*

(At the southern point with a yellow candle)

We pray for all those persons who have helped us and for those who have hurt or destroyed us.

(At the northern point with a white candle)

We give our thanks for the fecundity of all women who live on the planet Earth. Please send us the air, the rain and the sun for the fecundity of Mother Earth.

(At the center of the cross with a green candle and a blue candle for earth and sky)

Thank you for the hope you have given us, and for the center of the Earth.

Thank you, Heart of heaven, Heart of earth for the project of God: for creation—all of life; and for our grandmothers and grandfathers who have given us our Mayan spirituality.

Sister Cecilia Ruggiero, M.M.,
Argueta, Guatemala

Lord, we thank thee for this place in which we dwell;
for the love that unites us;
for the peace accorded us this day;
for the hope with which we expect the morrow;
for the health, the work, the food,
and the bright skies that make our lives delightful;
for our friends in all parts of the earth,
and our friendly helpers. Amen.

Robert Louis Stevenson

For the sparkle in the eyes of loved ones,
For the touch of a friendly hand
For the bread we eat
For the beautiful stars
For the roar of the breakers
For the Holy Word you have spoken to us
For the chance to be and do
We thank You O Lord our God. Amen.

Marie Iadavaia,
Bronxville, New York,
a friend of Maryknoll,
from a Christopher prayer of thanks

O blessed Lord, who has commanded us to love one another, grant us grace that having received your undeserved bounty, we may love everyone in you and for you. We pray for your clemency for everyone, but especially for the friends whom your love has given us. Love them, O fountain of love, and make them love you with all their heart, that they may will and speak and do those things only which are pleasing to you.

St. Anselm (1033–1109)

Thanksgiving

Principal: God, Father of our ancestors,
friend in our midst,
your children come before you,
Here is your food!
Here is your drink!
These things are yours before they are ours.
Now we are making a feast,
but it is thanksgiving;
we are thanking God.

Concelebrants:

O God, we and our ancestors
thank you and rejoice.
This food—
we shall eat it in your honor.
This drink—
we shall drink it in your honor.

Principal: We thank you for giving us life.

All: We thank you!

Principal: We thank you for giving us freedom.

All: We thank you!

Principal: We thank you for bringing us peace.

All: We thank you!

Principal: We thank you for him who bears the punishment that is our due.

All: We thank you!

Principal: For him on whom fell the punishment that brought us peace.

All: We thank you!

Epiclesis

Concelebrants:

> Father, send the Spirit of life,
> the Spirit of power and fruitfulness.
> With his breath, speak your Word into these things;
> make them the living body
> and the lifeblood
> of Jesus our brother.
> Give us who eat and drink in your presence life and power and fruitfulness of heart and body.
> Give us true brotherhood [and sisterhood] with your Son.

> On the night of his suffering
> he gave thanks for the bread
> which he held in his hands.
> This bread he shared among his followers, saying:
> all of you, take this, eat this:
> It is my body which will be handed over for you.

All: It is the body!

Concelebrants:

Then he shared drink with them saying:
all of you, take this, drink this:
It is my blood,
the blood of the pact of brotherhood
which begins now
and lasts forever.
This blood will be poured out for you and all
men
so that sins may be taken away.
Do this and remember me.

All: It is the blood!

Principal: Let us proclaim the mystery of faith:

All: Hail, hail, hail,
death, resurrection
and return,
may happiness come!

Concelebrants:

Lord, you are resurrection and life.
You, crucifixion, are here!
You, resurrection, are here!
You, ascension, are here!
You, spirit-medicine of life, are here!

Concelebrants:

Father, bring us life;
give us kinship
with all the children of God,
with the elders and forebears of your people,
with the living
and with the living-dead,
with children yet unborn,
in Jesus, who was anointed with the medicine
of life.

Doxology

All: And you our prayer,
               prayer of the long distant past,
               you, ancient Word, spoken by the Father,
               you whose breath is the Spirit,
               prayer of the ancestors,
               you are spoken now!
               Amen.

Father Joseph Healey, M.M.,
Dar es Salaam, Tanzania,
from the All Africa Eucharistic Prayer

Presence

Some people enter our lives
   like deer
   slipping in and out of the woods.
They touch our earth
   and as we stop
   to look at them
   they disappear as quietly as they came.
But we feel blessed
   for having experienced their gentle presence.
And we give you thanks
   that the world is a better place
   because of the joy that they brought.

Ellie Hays, Maryknoll Affiliate,
Sparks, Nevada, from a prayer
by Sister Joan Metzner, M.M.

Lord Jesus,
> teach us to live life fully each day
> to live it from
> the deepest center of our being
> to learn from everything
> and everyone
> most of all, to be grateful.

Father Michael D. Bassano, M.M.,
Bangkok, Thailand

Prayer for the United States

Lord, I speak to you with gratitude. On every side I see abundant blessings You have given to our country. Even when we face sorrow and sufferings, our burdens are light in the human family. Increase in us, Lord, the gift of faith so that all might see all people as your sons and daughters. Don't let us be blind to our fellowship in Christ because of the different color of our skin. Don't let us become deaf to your command of love because of our different political systems. Don't let us become isolated in fear of one another because of race or creed or difference of age.

Let us whom you have blessed so abundantly reach out and touch with generosity the lives of the poor. Give us the courage to help our mighty nation to use its power to bring freedom and dignity to all people. Help each of us, whoever and wherever we are, to realize that our lives may be the only copy of the Gospels many ever read. Amen.

Richard Philippone, Oak Ridge, Tennessee,
a friend of Maryknoll

How Wonderful It Is

How wonderful it is to be alive,
to go to town and buy a soda, in peace and without fear,
and then return home to see one's mother happy,
to be in El Salvador,
to have hands, eyes, feet,
to have friends who visit you,
to have a garden,
to have shoes,
to have faith in God,
to have a catechist.

How wonderful are
my father and mother
our church and community
our country
Jesus of Nazareth
the Virgin Mary

How wonderful is God!

Father Paul Belliveau, M.M.,
San Pedro Sula, Honduras,
from the writing of refugee children
from El Salvador, 1987

Father, you have sent many people in my life to direct me toward you. Thank you for all of them. May their lives be blessed with your presence always, as you have always blessed mine with theirs.

Celso S. Bate, Mandaluyong City, Philippines,
a friend of Maryknoll,
a prayer reflection during a visit to China

My Family

Of all the blessings you
Have bestowed upon me,
Heavenly Father, none is more
Precious than my family.

Thank you for the privilege of
Having my parents, siblings,
Spouse and children in joyful
Times and times of sorrow.

I beseech you to watch over all
Of us, living and departed. Grant
Us your divine benevolence. Help
Us to grow together in love, in
Imitation of the Holy Family, so
That one day we may all abide
At home with you.

A Maryknoll Lay Associate

Give Us Daily Awareness

On life's busy thoroughfares
We meet with angels unawares—
So, Father, make us kind and wise
So we may always recognize
The blessings that are ours to take,
The friendships that are ours to make
If we but open our heart's door wide
To let the sunshine of love inside.

Bill McCuen, Doylestown, Ohio,
a friend of Maryknoll

Deo Gratias

Thanks be to God for his goodness to me.
Thanks be to God now and in eternity.
Thanks be to God for the wonders he has done.
Thanks be to God for his dear and only son.
Thanks be to God for our sweet virgin mother.
Thanks be to God for becoming our brother.
Thanks be to God for his body and his blood.
Thanks be to God for this legacy of love.
Thanks be to God for his sacred heart benign.
Thanks be to God for this treasure divine.
Thanks be to God for my angel guardian bright.
Thanks be to God for morning, noon and night.
Thanks be to God in all ages and all climes.
Thanks be to God one hundred thousand times.
Thanks be to God in my joy and in my sorrow.
Thanks be to God for today and for tomorrow.
Thanks be to God in my illness and my health.
Thanks be to God both in poverty and in wealth.
Thanks be to God at my work and at my prayers.
Thanks be to God in my troubles and in my cares.
Thanks be to God in my life and at my death.
Thanks be to God when drawing my last breath.
And when, lifeless, my poor heart shall lie under the sod,
may my soul sing in heaven,
Thanks be to Thee, O good and generous God.

*Robert P. Hopkins, Ardsley, Pennsylvania,
a friend of Maryknoll, a favorite prayer
of a 108-year-old woman he visited
as a eucharistic minister.
She said it from memory.*

Holy Thursday–
A Struggle to Live and to Verbalize My Faith

Today is Holy Thursday and the refugees and I celebrated mass in our chapel, a large wooden building with a dirt floor and wooden benches. My task was to answer the question: What does Holy Thursday mean to a people who have suffered so much? Before some one thousand people, I washed the feet of twelve refugees. Their feet were dirty, because many wore no shoes. When I arrived at Felicita, I looked up and said to her: "It's an honor for me to wash your feet." Felicita is 62 years old and has great faith and hope in Jesus in spite of having seen her husband and four children killed in El Salvador. Then during my homily, I gave thanks:

For having received an invitation to sit with the refugees at the table of Jesus and receive his body and blood, and allow him to wash my feet.

For the God of life, who continues to create and maintain my life, and all life.

For the God of Exodus, who, today, continues to hear the cry of the poor, and enters into our history in order to liberate and lead us to the promised land.

For the God of Jesus, who is not a God of fire and vengeance, not a guerrilla, not a soldier of Central America who seeks to punish and destroy all opponents, but is a God of forgiveness, reconciliation, mercy, peace, and love.

For the death of Jesus, in my sister and brother refugees, who announces to the world that God's power is discovered in human weakness and God's victory comes through suffering and death.

For the resurrection of Jesus, in my sister and brother refugees, who proclaim a new life that conquers death, weariness, old age, and sickness.

Later, when I raised the chalice and paten high, in front of me I saw the faces of a multitude of poor farmers who have lost home, land, country, animals, family, liberty and dignity due to an unjust war. And they all answered "Amen!"

Father Paul Belliveau, M.M.,
San Pedro Sula, Honduras

Prayer of a Recovering Addict in North America

God, thank you for helping me find a way through my addiction and on to the path of recovery. I have been wandering and sick and joyless for too many years. You have heard my cry and given me the strength and courage to admit my powerlessness and to walk in a new way. I am beginning to feel hints of joy and enter into healthy relationships, especially with myself.

I know you will never leave me, God. In fact you have always been with me, in the midst of my pain and rejection. Now I awake each day and pray in thanksgiving for my being alive for one more day. My heart is grateful. Amen

Sister Mary Lou Herlihy, M.M., Bethany House,
Rochester, New York

Eventide

As the soft shadows of twilight play across the sky, I thank you, almighty Father, for bringing me safely through another day. I have tried to do your will, and I pray you will look kindly upon my efforts. I will rest now, relax my burdens and enjoy these waning hours. Please grant me refreshing sleep and the blessing of a new dawn.

A Maryknoll Missioner

For flowers that bloom about our feet,
For tender grass so fresh and sweet,
For song of bird and hum of bee,
Father in Heaven, we thank Thee!

For blue of stream, for blue of sky,
For pleasant shade of branches high,
For beauty of the blowing trees,
Father in Heaven, we thank Thee!

For mother love,
and father care,
brothers strong
and sisters fair,
Father in heaven,
we thank thee!

Peter Duncan, Bristol, Connecticut,
a friend of Maryknoll,
a prayer by Ralph Waldo Emerson

For the Church

I give you thanks, Father, for blessing every day; for being with us in every moment of our lives; for giving us our daily bread; for keeping me close to you. Thank you, Lord, for giving us, in your Holy Church, a preparation with your Word, which fills me with much happiness, being always with this living word that you give us through many persons who make possible your call to all of us, Father, by your sacrifice for all of us. Father Eternal. Amen.

Sister Joan Uhlen, M.M.,
Chacraseca, Nicaragua,
a prayer of Sayda Ojeda Salazar
(translated by Sister Bernice Kita, M.M.)

Holy Creator Spirit,
you have left signs of your love for us throughout the
        Universe,
the starry heavens, deep oceans, singing birds, green grow-
        ing plants,
life-giving waters,
majestic mountains, fertile valleys.
You have birthed a home for all living creatures on the
        Earth and we feel
wonder at the
precious gift of life.

Today, we gather together—united in spirit with this great
        cosmic community
to rejoice and give thanks,
to heal and let go,
to enter the dark and deep mysteries,
to share the news,
to break the bread of the Universe and drink the living
        waters of the
Cosmos itself
in all its divinity.

Let our worship make us strong.
And may we express our lasting gratitude to you by the
        lives we live,
called to be co-creators with you of the future. Amen.

Sister Rose Marie Cecchini, M.M.,
Gallup, New Mexico

Workday's End

As this workday draws to a close, Lord, I reflect with satisfaction on my accomplishments. Thank you for giving me the opportunity to do honorable work.

Where I succeeded in being a true Christian, I am grateful. Where I failed, I beg your forgiveness. I will not dwell on the work left undone, for with your grace, I will be here tomorrow to begin anew. In work, as in life, let me always see the cup as half full, rather than half empty.

A Maryknoll Missioner

Lord, Holy Father, I give you infinite thanks for all the marvels you give us in every moment. When I go to sleep and close my eyes, when I am praying to you, I see your face, Lord. How happy I am at those moments, and every hour that I see you, like a divine light. When I am working and when I am sleeping, I feel you close to me.

Thank you, Lord, because you hear my prayer. Thank you, Father, for everything. Lord, if you want me to be your catechist, here I am, Lord, at your disposal. I thank you that I feel you in my heart. Glory to you, and to your son, Jesus, and your Holy Spirit. Amen.

Sister Joan Uhlen, M.M.,
Chacraseca, Nicaragua,
a prayer of Juana Gutiérrez
(translated by Sister Bernice Kita, M.M.)

— THE PRAYER JESUS TAUGHT US —

"When you pray . . . go to your inner room, close the door, and pray to your Father in secret. And your Father who sees in secret will repay you. . . . Your Father knows what you need before you ask him.

"This is how you are to pray:

Our Father in heaven,
    hallowed be your name,
        your kingdom come,
    your will be done,
        on earth as in heaven.
        Give us today our daily bread;
        and forgive us our debts,
        as we forgive our debtors;
        and do not subject us to the final test,
        but deliver us from the evil one."

MATTHEW 6:5–12

Amen!

List of Contributors